THRIFTSTYLE

THRIFTSTYLE

THE ULTIMATE BARGAIN SHOPPER'S GUIDE TO SMART FASHION

ALLISON ENGEL, REISE MOORE
AND MARGARET ENGEL

PHOTOGRAPHS BY **ROGER SNIDER**

imagine!

A BUNKER HILL STUDIO BOOK

An Imagine Book
Published by Charlesbridge
85 Main Street
Watertown, MA 02472
(617) 926-0329
www.imaginebooks.net

This book was designed and produced by
Bunker Hill Studio Books LLC
285 River Road, Piermont, NH 03779.
Telephone 603 272 9221   info@bunkerhillstudiobooks.com

Library of Congress Cataloging-in-Publication Data
Names: Engel, Allison, author. | Moore, Reise, author. | Engel, Margaret, author.
Title: Thriftstyle : the ultimate bargain shopper's guide to smart fashion /
Allison Engel, Reise Moore and Margaret Engel ; photographs by Roger Snider.
Description: Watertown, MA : Imagine, 2017. | "A Bunker Hill Studio Book."
Identifiers: LCCN 2016039395 (print) | LCCN 2016058540 (ebook) |
ISBN 9781623545024 (paperback) | ISBN 9781632892027 (ebook) |
ISBN 9781632892034 (ebook pdf)
Subjects: LCSH: Shopping. | Consignment sale shops. | Fashion. | BISAC:
DESIGN / Fashion. | SOCIAL SCIENCE / Popular Culture.
Classification: LCC TX335 .E466 2017 (print) | LCC TX335 (ebook) |
DDC 381/.1—dc23
LC record available at https://lccn.loc.gov/2016039395

Printed in China
10 9 8 7 6 5 4 3 2 1

contents

introduction

Thrifting hits all the right buttons. It's good for the wallet,
good for the planet and good for your creative side.
—ALLISON ENGEL

If loving thrifting is wrong, I don't want to be right.
—REISE MOORE

As the sign says at the Stuff Etc consignment stores,
"Wear it like you paid full price."
—MARGARET ENGEL

Every last item you see modeled in this book is thrifted: clothes, shoes, jewelry, and accessories. Most items were purchased in 2015, a few days before our photo shoots. If we were lucky, we scored an extra-special bargain at the $2 and $3 clothing sales at Salvation Army and Goodwill.

In the course of this project, we visited more than 165 thrift stores in multiple states. For cool points, we would like to say we are battle worn after making our way through all these stores. But the truth is, it was an absolute pleasure. It was a thrill to hunt for the ideal pair of pumps for the green sequined dress we found for $2, or the right pair of men's trousers to match the bold boots we bought for $8.

As we shopped, digital pictures would fly among the authors via text message showing off a great find, soliciting a yea or nay on a so-so candidate or getting confirmation that one of us was right to walk away from a questionable choice. Thrifting is something anyone can learn to do successfully. It does not require a special eye or take endless amounts of time.

When we started this journey, the goal was to create the definitive guide to thrift shopping. Now we realize a journey into thrifting is about so much more. On the macro level, it is a multibillion-dollar nonprofit-based industry that accepts donations from everyday people, sells them on to consumers eager to save money on clothes, and uses the proceeds to fund missions that change lives for the better. On a global level, it also is about recycling, renewing, and keeping textile waste out of landfills. At the micro level, it is an activity in which we can discover our personal style while we support small, often family-owned businesses—the local cobbler, dry cleaner, tailor, reweaver. And it's about learning to master our clothes: how to repair them, clean them, wear them. All this happens while we become savvy shoppers, clued in to what makes up quality clothing and how to improve garments with creativity and imagination.

We hope there are several images and suggestions inside that will inspire you to visit your local thrift store—whether it is located across town or can be found by clicking on your phone—and invest in looking good while doing good.

All images are by photographer Roger Snider (rogersnider.com), except as noted.

THRIFTSTYLE

1

why thrifting
is thriving

Americans are drowning in clothing, which is one reason that there has never been a better time to shop for bargains in thrift stores.

Unlike many consumer goods, mass-produced clothing has gotten cheaper over the past few decades, fueled by the fast fashion phenomenon that has shoppers continually buying—and throwing away—garments. But it's not just poorly made trendy items that are on the racks at thrift, resale, and consignment shops. Our appetite for fashion at all levels—from infants to adults, and at all price points—means that high-quality and luxury labels, vintage finds, and brand-new merchandise with tags intact can be found at thrift stores everywhere—on your computer, on your phone, or inside brick and mortar shops.

America and the rest of the world are obsessed with fashion. When more than a quarter of a million people show up for New York Fashion

Week, a ritual repeated at other fashion weeks around the globe, and millions others check in on these shows online, the impact of the $3 trillion a year worldwide clothing industry becomes clear.

One consequence is that Americans now routinely buy more clothes than they actually wear. Instead of shopping seasonally four times a year, people in America now shop for clothes every week or every day. The result? Overstuffed closets and more donations to an ever-growing number of thrift stores.

Thrift stores in America are a market segment worth some $12 billion in yearly revenue, according to the Association of Resale Professionals, which says the number of thrift stores is rising 7 percent annually. Goodwill alone has more than three thousand retail outlets and reports more than $5.4 billion annually in revenue.

TheThriftShopper.com, one of many thrift store locator websites, estimates one in six adults now shops in resale stores.

The explosion of mobile apps for locating used designer and thrift merchandise is increasing that number. Once thrift stores were defined primarily by Goodwill, Salvation Army, St. Vincent de Paul, Value Village, and AMVETS, but now there are dozens of upscale thrift store chains, with amenities such as personal shoppers, phone apps, fashion blogs, loyalty discount programs, and daily digital finds. Large digital thrift communities are on social media, commenting on each other's resale purchases and generating personal friendships through meet-ups and frequent messages from buyer to seller.

This fitted and flared dress could pass for the designer Azzedine Alaïa, but was $4 at Desert Best Friend's Closet. The $3.99 handbag Marzen is holding is by Yokohama Takashimaya, and her booties, $8 (both Salvation Army).

Thrift stores are establishing communities in other ways, expanding their services to include offering free classes in learning English, computer skills, and crafts, especially in areas of the United States with many retirees and immigrants. Shuttle buses often bring in shoppers and volunteers from senior living centers. The growing popularity of thrifting means new stores are larger and handicapped-accessible, with some offering to pick up items from estates for free.

There's been double-digit growth in new resale chains, including Clothes Mentor, Plato's Closet, America's Thrift Stores, Stuff Etc, Unique Thrift, Savers, and Encore. The chains include Buffalo Exchange, which operates forty-eight stores in seventeen states, ringing up more than $72 million yearly. Some chains advertise on national television, hold makeovers and fashion shows, and have celebrity endorsers.

Two big resale franchisers, Winmark Corp. and NTY Franchise Co., both in Minnesota, have separate chains of stores for children's goods, teen clothing, young adult wear, and women's clothing. Winmark franchises 1,116 resale stores across the United States, with some fifty new stores planned annually, making it possible for

Regular thrift shopper Nora Kirkpatrick at Goodwill's flagship Los Angeles store in Atwater Village.

Blake's entirely thrifted outfit includes Italian wool pants, $3 (Goodwill); a vintage John Weitz cashmere blazer, $14.99 (Goodwill); and vintage gray Italian suede shoes with Pilgrim buckles purchased on eBay for $32.

MYTHS ABOUT THRIFTING

Like many industries, the resale business has been disrupted by the Internet, by chain ownership, by eBay, and by many other market forces. Today's modern thrift store looks nothing like the charity and mom-and-pop stores established after World War II, yet there are stubborn taboos that keep some potential shoppers away. Here are some common misconceptions about resale shopping, and our responses.

Myth: Clothes at thrift stores are worn out.

Reality: All donated clothes are sorted and evaluated; few garments with rips or stains make it onto the racks. Most clothes are donated because of life circumstances (a move, death, weight loss), not because someone's clothes have outrun their useful life.

Myth: A stranger wore the clothes, so they won't be clean.

Reality: This is a risk at most clothing stores, retail or resale, although few shoppers raise questions about the cleanliness of retail offerings. In 2010, *Good Morning America* bought new clothing items from stores in a variety of price ranges and had them tested by the director of microbiology and immunology at New York University. He found bacteria and heavy contamination on several items, likely because they

budget-conscious shoppers to cash in on their closet clutter by selling—not donating—their unwanted items.

Moving upward from fluorescent lighting and vinyl floors, there are tasteful thrift stores that mimic full-price retail outlets with chandeliers, plank floors, and inventory carefully arranged by size, style, era, designer, or color. There are funky boutiques, includ-

Devon wears a 1970s dress by Holly Harp, designer to rock stars, $8.99, with Kelsi Dagger over-the-knee suede boots, $8 (both Salvation Army).

had been repeatedly tried on. He recommended washing new items or putting them through one cycle in a hot dryer before wearing. He also recommended washing your hands after shopping—the same precautions we take and recommend for thrifted items.

Myth: Thrift stores should be reserved for the poor. If you shop there, you are limiting what's available for the disadvantaged to buy.

Reality: Charitable thrift stores need and welcome free-spending shoppers to support their missions, from food banks to worker training, helping disadvantaged youths, animal rescue, and more.

Myth: It's too hard to find things in a thrift store.

Reality: Stores of every size are upgrading their fixtures, lighting, dressing rooms, and product organization. Goodwill, among others, organizes garments by color, as well as by the divisions customary in department and discount stores. It is true that many stores don't have the manpower to also sort by size, although high-end resale shops generally do.

Myth: Thrift store clothing is unlovely and out-of-date.

Reality: Because of the regular turnover of goods in thrift stores, dated merchandise, if accepted at all, is quickly moved off racks to recyclers. Many donated items are of current fashion, some with original tags intact.

ing pop-ups doing business in Airstream trailers that park next to food trucks in college towns and urban neighborhoods.

Many stores have cleaned up their interiors, improved lighting, added dressing rooms and installed enticing displays and creative advertising. No longer tucked away in obscure shopping zones or church annexes, thrift stores can be found in prime locations. Case in point: in Minnetonka, Minnesota, there is a Goodwill store next to a Maserati dealership. Goodwill also hosted a secondhand fashion show fund-raiser at the Italian Embassy in Washington, D.C., complete with catwalk. After the show, guests shopped at a Goodwill pop-up shop.

Gentleman's Resale, on New York's Upper East Side.
Photo/Allison Engel

There are now high-end consignment shops just for men in Chicago, New York, Los Angeles, and elsewhere.

Many locales have wedding and maternity-only consignment shops. There are also shops across the country selling used children's furniture, second-hand sporting goods, and estate jewelry.

The increased interest in thrifting has even generated an unofficial national holiday, the National Second-hand Wardrobe Day, on August 25. Recycling, reusing, and repurposing clothing also has prompted Eco Fashion Week, held annually in Vancouver since 2010.

Researching this book, the three of us visited more than 165 thrift stores coast-to-coast. Our travels took us to nineteen states, and we enjoyed seeing regional differences and shopping in all sorts of locales, from the Hospital Thrift Shop in Nantucket, Massachusetts; the Children's Hospital of the King's Daughters Thrift Store in Kitty Hawk, North Carolina; Fifi's Fine Resale Apparel in Venice, Florida; the Salvation Army in Newton, Iowa; and Savers in Berkeley, California.

We found interesting items and bargains at all. Technology helps thrift shoppers, who can easily

Richard wears a $10 Jhane Barnes shirt made from fabric woven in Japan, $10 (Collectors Corner); Italian wool pants, $3 (Goodwill); and authentic Mark Astbury Beatle boots from Liverpool, England, $19.99 (Goodwill).

(1) Goodwill, Rockville, Maryland; (2) Savers, Berkeley, California; (3) Secondi, Washington, D.C.; (4) Children's Hospital of the King's Daughters Thrift Store, Kitty Hawk, North Carolina; (5) Union Rescue Mission Thrift Store, Covina, California; (6) Reddz Trading, Bethesda, Maryland; (7) Goodwill, La Quinta, California; (8) Children's Hospital of the King's Daughters, Wilmington, North Carolina; (9) Hospital Thrift Shop, Nantucket, Massachusetts. *All photos/Allison Engel*

search online for specific items, sizes, and brands. At ThriftTown stores in California, New Mexico, and Texas, executive Wendy Steinmetz is seeing shoppers with smartphones or tablets in hand searching for items to duplicate their favorite Pinterest and Instagram looks. "Pin it and go and thrift it," Steinmetz said, who notes there's now a hashtag of #PinnedItandThriftedIt where shoppers upload photos of their success in duplicating looks they see on runway models and advertisements.

The big chains offer online shopping and auctions (usually with some of their better merchandise), mobile apps, and blogs, including some in Spanish. Start-ups are bringing fresh technology-driven approaches. ThredUp, founded by three Harvard MBAs, is intent on transforming the clothing consignment industry by making the process easy, digital, and financially rewarding. The company sells more than 25,000 brands of like-new women's and kid's clothing, shipping purchases to customers in fancy tissue-wrapped boxes. To make the process of selling clothing easy, ThredUp sends bags to people who want to sell their clothing. At the company's headquarters in San Francisco and in San Leandro, California, employees sort hundreds of clothing bags each day. The company motto is: "To inspire a new generation of consumers to think secondhand first."

Flower girl Christiahn loved her DV by Dolce Vita shoes with sparkly heels from ThredUp, $10.69. Her Children brand dress was $5.99 (Salvation Army).

ThredUp and others are tapping into the Generation Xers, millennials, and teens who gave the song "Thrift Shop" by Macklemore & Ryan Lewis hundreds of millions of YouTube views and many spin-offs.

There are now dozens of thrifting blogs, with titles like *Tales from the Thrift* and *Vintage*

Silk Julie Francis dress, $7.99 (Goodwill); Tahari shoes, $12 (Clothes Mentor); Modell Royal crocodile handbag, $14.99 (Salvation Army); heavy black bead necklace, $9.99 (Goodwill).

Vandalizm. One, *Fashion Hound*, focuses on reducing our fashion footprint with the mantra "reuse, reinvent, reduce" and declares: "Second-hand never has to mean second best."

As thrift shopping loses its dowdy image, the social stigma also is fading.

After the recession hit in 2008, *USA TODAY* found that seventy percent of the adults it surveyed said buying used items was now more socially acceptable.

"Haul" videos uploaded to the Internet have become popular. They feature thrifters who have filmed their shopping finds, gleefully announcing the bargain-priced items they've snared.

When *The Chicago Tribune* featured columnist Ellen Warren's thrift store score—a pristine pair of Manolo Blahnik navy heels for $6.99 (original price $450)—it trumpeted the news on its front page. Her "diamond in the rhinestone bin" find generated an avalanche of phone calls, e-mails, letters, and a parade of shoppers in fancy cars to "her" store who had never before considered a trip to a thrift store.

The new popularity of thrift shopping is driven by factors other than faster fashion cycles. There are more recession-scarred bargain hunters, for one, including shoppers of all ages who long for quality but can't pay the sky-high prices for many designer goods. As the quality of moderately priced clothing has diminished, "Goodwill hunting" has become more appealing. One resale shop, Women's Closet Exchange, in

Cristy wears a Jody of California dress, $4.99, and Braetan wool coat, $9.99 (both Salvation Army). Over-the-knee suede boots, $20 (It's a Bargain Thrift Shop).

ARE THERE ANY BARGAINS LEFT?

Is all this new attention and foot traffic to thrift stores making treasures harder to come by? Frequently we hear the lament that "thrift stores are all picked over" and "you can't find the good stuff anymore."

That is so not true. As regular thrifters, we find bargains on high-end clothing every time we shop. It's rare that we don't find brand-new items, still with their tags.

And the Vinnies (St. Vincent de Paul), Salvos (Salvation Army), and G-Wahs (Goodwill) stores don't have to be located in pricey neighborhoods.

For example, recently we stopped at a Goodwill in Fontana, California, a middle-class city in the Inland Empire east of Los Angeles. We spent half an hour in the store and came away with the following:

A new jacket with a $119.50 price tag from Aéropostale still attached was $19.99 at Goodwill. (Photo/Allison Engel)

A mint-condition, heavy, red, cotton men's Façonnable jacket for $8.99; a Jaeger of London viscose and wool women's black and white fully-lined blazer with interesting tabs at the lapel and waist in perfect condition for $7.99; a like-new St. John striped knit wool and rayon sleeveless striped tunic in dark brown and cream for $3.99; a purple cable knit cropped top that was acrylic but was the ideal size and color to match a skirt we had, for $1.99; a Hugo Boss 100 percent cotton men's checked long-sleeved shirt with spread collar—also an item we had been searching for to go with a particular suit, for $5.99; and a stunning chartreuse sleeveless silk shirtwaist by Dana B.

St. Louis, says it best: "We're the secret to dressing like a million bucks . . . without spending it."

Other reasons for the surge in thrifting include the enduring fashion cachet of vintage clothing, the environmental interest in reuse and

and Karen for $7.99. It was in perfect condition save missing its belt—something that was easily remedied with a thrifted long silk scarf.

The total for the six items was $36.94. Subtracting our 10 percent senior discount (given to anyone fifty-five years or older and also to all military personnel, no matter what age), the final bill was $33.24—less than the cost of purchasing any single one of the items new, with the possible exception of the acrylic crop top.

Since the Internet allows anyone to Google a label and find out the retail price of an item, it might follow that thrift stores price their clothing based on that information. We have not found that to be the case.

We've found St. John items for close to $100 in thrift stores, and for less than $10, like this knit top we found in North Carolina. *(Photo/Allison Engel)*

Prices for high-end items vary widely. On the same day we bought the St. John knit top for a final price of $3.59, we found St. John items in another thrift store going for $80 and up. Eighty dollars is still a bargain for St. John clothing, but it's hard to think about shelling out eight tens when you can find the same thing for less than $10 in other thrift stores.

Day in and day out, we have run across eye-popping bargains. Once, shopping at the Unclaimed Baggage Center in Scottsboro, Alabama, where major airlines sell unclaimed suitcase contents for pennies per pound, we found a genuine Louis Vuitton hanging bag for $5 and a string of luxury pearls, with its hallmark "M" on the clasp, for $30. As a friend noted, "They didn't know Mikimoto from Mickey Mouse."

recycling, the "slow clothes" movement to counter fast fashion, and a new generation of DIY sewers, leather crafters, quilters, and knitters who "upcycle" and repurpose clothing. Above all, there is the time-honored thrill of the hunt.

You may have heard the story in 2015 about the sweater once owned by famed Green Bay Packers footballcoach Vince Lombardi that was bought by a Knoxville, Tennessee, couple for 58 cents. They bought it at an Asheville, North Carolina, Goodwill outlet where items are sold by the pound. It was later sold by Heritage Auctions for $43,020.

Thrift stores allow shoppers of all income levels to engage in the great American pastime of treasure hunting.

Bus tours in San Diego, Atlanta, and Nashville cater to thrift shoppers looking to canvass the best stores with knowledgeable guides. A group of Atlanta thrift store fans are part of Thrifting Atlanta, with 19,269 members who trade tips on stores, style bargains, and how to authenticate designer goods. Second-hand shopping tours are plentiful in New York City, Palm Beach, Florida, and other high-income areas.

Regular thrift shoppers quickly learn about military, college, and senior citizen discounts; stores that price everything for $2 or $3 during certain weekends; and places that offer $10 fill-a-bag shopping promotions. Online stores often offer 15 to 40 percent discounts for your first order.

Stacey's silk Milly dress looks like the 1960s, $7.99 (Goodwill); Anne Klein spectator pumps, $22 (Clothes Mentor); Rodo Italy handbag, $7.99 (Salvation Army).

Not only is shopping at thrift stores good for the wallet, but there are noble reasons to thrift. India Salvor Menuez, a top model, said she only shops secondhand. "It's better for the planet," she told *Town & Country.*

Other models, actresses, musicians, and celebrities increasingly talk about and are photographed wearing treasured pieces of used designer clothing. Many celebrities and stylists openly sell their dresses and handbags online, with special "shop my closet" features on high-end resale sites.

Comedian Amy Schumer endorses Goodwill's efforts to bring working wardrobes to needy women in Los Angeles. Beyoncé and her mom, Tina, also are ardent Goodwill supporters and encourage giving by setting up donation boxes at concert venues. Designer Stella McCartney and the Clean by Design program, launched by the Natural Resources Defense Council, include thrifting in their push for ecologically responsible fashion.

Depending on the store, sale signs change weekly or daily. *Photo/Allison Engel*

Changing attitudes toward secondhand garments are taking hold in other countries as well. As *The New York Times* noted in a feature on a Singapore vintage shop, "the shopping culture here has shifted as women have warmed up to western attitudes regarding wearing used clothing."

Fast fashion may provide shoppers an opportunity for splurging, but the cost to the environment and the overworked, low-wage, primarily female garment workers is large.

Books such as *Wear No Evil* (by Greta Eagan) and *To Die For: Is Fashion Wearing Out the World?* (by Lucy Siegle) document the damage that fast fashion has on labor markets and the environment.

"As any economist will tell you, cheaper prices stimulate consumption, and the current low rate of fashion has spurred a shopping free-for-all, where we are buying and hoarding roughly 20 billion garments *per year* as a nation," notes Elizabeth Cline in her book, *Overdressed: The Shockingly High Cost of Cheap Fashion.*

Instead of buying cheap new fashions for pocket change, it's better for our natural resources for us to spend the same small amounts of cash for used clothing. You can indulge more responsibly.

It is estimated that there are billions of dollars of unworn clothing in American homes. This is not just a problem for shopaholics and hoarders. It affects our homes and how we live our lives.

A book on de-cluttering, *The Life-Changing Magic of Tidying Up*, by Marie Kondo, became a blockbuster, selling 3 million copies worldwide, prompting her to write a second bestseller on organizing. Offloading no longer loved items, for tax purposes or cash, was one Kondo solution. Thrift, vintage, and consignment shops were the beneficiaries of her life-simplifying advice.

Fans of Tim Gunn, the fashion professor who stars in *Project Runway*, are familiar with his adage to practice good self-discipline and regularly clean your closets. "New York is a blessing in a way,"

Sign on truck at Nu4U Thrift Store in Rancho Mirage, California.
Photo/Allison Engel

he wrote in his book, *The Natty Professor*, "because we live in smaller spaces than much of the rest of the nation, and that helps us think about our clothes with an editing eye. . . . With clothing or objects, if something comes in, something has to go."

Reselling has never been easier. Vinted, a free mobile app, which claims 2 million monthly users, gives customers opportunities to empty and refill their closets by uploading photos and descriptions of clothing they want to buy, sell, or swap. It has plenty of company in the speed thrift space, with Tradesy, Threadflip, and many others.

Major chains such as Plato's Closet and Clothes Mentor give sellers cash on the spot, with no appointment. Just fill a laundry basket with clean, folded, on-trend classic or timeless clothes and show up, prospective sellers are told.

Recycling and reusing are critical, because too many of America's soft goods end up in landfills.

Textile waste—clothes, footwear, towels, bedding, and drapery being discarded instead of recycled or resold—accounts for 10.5 million tons of landfill trash yearly in the United States. Only 15 percent of clothing in America is recycled, according to the Council for Textile Recycling, and this is one of the poorest recycling rates for reusable goods. And our discarded clothing pile is growing, the council warns. In 1999 we threw away 18.2 billion pounds of textiles. By 2009 the figure was 25.46 billion pounds. By 2019 it is estimated that our textile waste will be 35.4 billion pounds.

Bales of clothing behind a Savers thrift store in Berkeley, California.
Photo/Allison Engel

"Everything became disposable," laments Todd Thelen, proprietor of Artifacts, a vintage clothing and furniture store in Iowa City. He has two professional pickers help stock his store, but he is finding it harder to locate quality clothing. "Everything's from Walmart and there's so much of it."

Realizing that our overstuffed closets represent cash, charities of all descriptions are more actively soliciting castoffs. Thrift stores run by hospital auxiliaries, churches, synagogues, and other charities are becoming more professional and attracting more shoppers.

By patronizing thrift stores we contribute to a multitude of charities that help men and women with substance abuse recovery, people reentering society after prison, animal rescue, and other good causes. You can help others through shopping and donating clothes. At Goodwill, for

LEFT: Many donation boxes are for nonprofit enterprises. *Photo/Allison Engel*; RIGHT: Well-known thrifts, such as Salvation Army, are competing for curbside donations with new donation bins springing up from companies that may or may not be nonprofits. *Photo/David Mathias*

example, even as the organization updates and expands shops, officials emphasize that the organization's focus is squarely on its mission of transforming lives and providing meaningful employment, not being a major retailer. Selling clothing is simply a means to its humanitarian end.

Technology makes it easy to donate clothing to charities. At the National Council of Jewish Women—Los Angeles' eBay site, for example, you upload an item photo, set a price, and choose what percentage of the sale you want to send to the charity. When the item sells, the donor mails it to the purchaser. eBay has a multitude of charities using this method to turn donors' clothing into cash, all without donors having to drop off items at a store.

As more nonprofits join the ranks of resellers, it's important to ask questions of the stores you shop and of the companies that collect your donations. You may not share the values or religious beliefs of some nonprofits, and that may influence your decisions on where to shop or donate. Be aware that some charities have licensed their names to for-profit clothing collection companies. The charity may only get a fraction of the proceeds. The New York Attorney General, in one case, found a

Yonkers clothing bin company was operating a "fraudulent charitable solicitation scheme" by giving charities only a small portion of the $10 million it earned by reselling donated clothes.

Many new clothing bin companies are for-profit entities, and their boxes are sprouting up on sidewalks, at gas stations, and in parking lots across the country, confusing donators who mistakenly assume that all clothing bins are placed by nonprofits.

Shoppers often are surprised by the low prices on high-end goods, which is part of the seduction of thrift shopping. But unlike used cars, houses, and boats, there are no established prices for secondhand clothing. The Association of Resale Professionals (NARTS), based in St. Clair Shores, Michigan, which has more than 1,100 members, notes that the operations of its resellers vary widely in size, prices, and offerings. It follows that the fashion and brand knowledge of those putting price tags on items are similarly varied.

The association, which counsels members on best business practices,

The fine print on the boxes can reveal that your donations go to a for-profit business. *Photos/Allison Engel*

also addresses the issue of fake designer goods on its website, narts.org. It passes along advice from the International AntiCounterfeiting Coalition, which gives commonsense tips ("avoid blurred or torn labels," "keep an eye out for product names that are misspelled or altered"), and so forth. More usefully, the association's site gives links for reporting retailers selling fake goods and for finding authentication services for luxury goods.

Another solution is to seek out resellers who vet their designer goods. One, the WebThriftStore, has thirty charity partners that take in donations from around the country. The items on the site are not inexpensive—$99 Fendi flats—but they're in top condition, and you can sort for what you're looking for in a matter of clicks.

Goodwill.com also authenticates its designer handbags, from a Jimmy Choo leather bag for $90 to a Dooney & Bourke hobo bag for $28. If you're among the 3 million people shopping on the ultra high-end website Vestiaire Collective, housed in Paris, rest assured that its second-hand goods are authenticated by a dozen quality inspectors.

The mania for designer goods and one-of-a-kind garments and accessories has sparked many knowledgeable buyers to set up shop on eBay and other Internet sites. Rachel Ericsen, who works for an Oakland, California, estate sale firm, Dan May Estate Liquidation Services, often resells pieces of valuable clothing, such as vintage jeans, that she identifies from sorting through closets and boxes of clothes from homes the firm is emptying.

"My best find was a pair of Big 'E' Levis, which sold for $1,500 on eBay," she relates. "Nineteen-fifties T-shirts and sweatshirts are big. The best old things have tags sewn in, never printed in. You never know what you'll find—Pucci scarves, fur coats, even homemade stuff like normal housedresses from the 1940s."

Collectors make some brands gold in the resale market. The Lululemon brand of exercise wear, for example, has obsessive fans who buy scarce, used leggings and tops from hundreds of groups on Facebook and eBay that are devoted to reselling items of this brand.

Other sellers of used items don't go near eBay or other Internet sites and do just fine. Dave Mayer, the owner of the Millsboro Bazaar, housed since 1989 in a former funeral home in Millsboro, Delaware, has made a career of selling vintage costume jewelry in a shop that has been praised as the best in the country.

His shop features thousands of pieces meticulously organized by manufacturer, color, and era. The inventory is so large and well organized that customers come in to match missing pieces. Shoppers for proms, weddings, and holiday gifts appreciate the one-of-a-kind statement made by necklaces, clip earrings, and hard-to-find pieces from designers such as Miriam Haskell. He says, "There's never been a stigma in buying used jewelry. When the economy tanks, we do better."

Mayer notes that the best-designed jewelry and vintage clothes and accessories he carries last for decades. The styles come back into fashion repeatedly.

Our aim in *ThriftStyle* is to help readers find these worthy bargains and learn how to reclaim and renew fashion treasures. In the next chapters, we'll tell you how to edit stores' sometime overwhelming inventories, discover clues to quality, learn how to refresh and rework secondhand items, and how to embellish plain garments, turning them from drab to fab. We'll show you thrifting in action, solving common fashion problems. Advice from fashion and clothing professionals—"What the Pros Know"—is included, as well as helpful size charts, lists of thrifting websites, videos and blogs, store locators, and other shopping aids.

navigating the store

Even as some thrift stores become mainstream and adopt some of the trappings of boutiques and department stores, your average resale shop is not likely to be mistaken for a full-priced retail store. Full-priced stores will often have soundtracks to create a certain mood, carefully designed lighting to enhance the visual experience, and artful displays to maximize sales. High-end stores work hard to engage the senses, creating a unique brand experience that defines their sense of "cool."

In contrast, the defining visual of the thrift store experience is one of clothes everywhere. Music is often local radio with too-familiar pop songs playing at a healthy volume. The lights add no particular punch other than to keep you from running into the racks. And although most stores will sort by type of clothes (men's, women's, children, outerwear, etc.) and some stores may sort by color, it is rare to see inventory also sorted by size. Shoppers may be faced with rows of racks, bins, and rounders stuffed with a hodge-podge of clothing.

So how do you make sense of the clutter and cut a store down to size? We have a multitude of suggestions.

✱ First, don't judge a store by its exterior. We found a full-length Ultrasuede coat in mint condition for $3 and many European high-end labels at a store in a dicey neighborhood that looked unpromising from the outside.

We almost passed on entering the store because it looked so sketchy from the street. Inside, the inventory organization was chaotic, but the place had wonderful finds—at prices below Salvation Army and Goodwill, which is saying something. While it is true that ritzier neighborhoods usually have better quality castoffs, we have found top-notch clothing and surprising finds in all types of neighborhoods.

✱ Shop with a specific item or two in mind (or on a shopping list) to help you focus. Having a

Thrift store "outlets" pile items, unsorted, in large bins. Shopping in these places can be tough even for the pros. Customers are charged by weight, not by item.
Photo/Allison Engel

Sophia wears a bargain Ultrasuede coat, $3 (Central Thrift); a J. Crew skirt, $2 (Salvation Army); silk blouse, $4 (Desert Best Friend's Closet); Vince Camuto shoes, $8 (Salvation Army).

SHOP FOR MONOCHROMATIC GRAYS

FROM LEFT: **(1)** Blake in a John Weitz cashmere blazer, $14.99; Italian wool pants, $5.99; Geoffrey Beene shirt, $3; gray belt, $2.70 (all from Goodwill); Byford wool vest, $10 (Discovery Thrift); silk tie, $1 (Central Thrift); by Skipper vintage Italian shoes, $32 (Etsy). **(2)** A second monochromatic look for Blake includes Prada slacks, $3, (Goodwill); Peter Raney Hong Kong Tailors sport coat, $2 (Salvation Army); Coronado side zip ankle boots, $19.99 (Goodwill); silk tie, $2 (Hospice Resale Boutique); Calvin Klein shirt, $3 (Goodwill). **(3)** Shirley does all gray in a Banana Republic dress, $7.99; Fioni cloth heels, $8.99 (both Goodwill); beaded bracelet, $2.50; vintage silver necklace, $3 (both Salvation Army). **(4)** Irina is monochromatic in a Elizabeth and James leather vest, $15; Banana Republic boots, $5; cashmere sweater, $3.99; "jade" necklace, $5 (all Salvation Army); wool kilt, $4.99 (Goodwill).

specific color you are looking for can narrow the store, particularly if the racks are color-coordinated. If you are new to thrifting and aren't sure what you want, think about selecting a favorite color and trying to put together a monochromatic outfit. Picking up on the trend of using gray as a go-to neutral, we thrifted outfits for men and women and found the shopping went much faster than if we simply browsed the racks for anything that caught our eyes. We snagged a pair of gray Prada pants

• If you favor unique items, be aware that thrift stores carry inventory you won't find in most department stores or boutiques, such as hand-sewn or -knitted items; costumes from plays and dance recitals; custom Halloween costumes; gently worn wedding and bridesmaid's dresses; random corporate and company uniforms complete with decals, embroidered logos, and (sometimes) names; sports jerseys; event T-shirts; and jackets, vintage clothes packed away for years, and clothing from other parts of the world bought by tourists or people moving here. They also carry new items, garments from store closings, and manufacturers' samples.

• Consider looking in furniture consignment and antique stores. Both often have small amounts of clothing and jewelry for sale, and it is often vintage.

• Ask your shoe repair shop, dry cleaners, reweavers, and tailors if they have unclaimed items for sale. Some of these shops donate the items no one picks up, but some will sell them. The bonus is that they have already been repaired and cleaned.

Thrift shops aren't the only place to find secondhand items. Shoes that patrons never picked up are for sale at a shoe repair shop. *Photo/ Allison Engel*

in our model's size, a vintage John Weitz gray cashmere blazer from the defunct Woodward & Lothrop department store in Washington, D.C., and our choice of half a dozen gray ties at each thrift store we visited. On a lark, we put "gray men's shoes" into the search engines of eBay

"NOT MY DEPARTMENT" TIPS

The magic and fun of thrift shopping is found in reinvention. Yes, you can walk in and shop the women's section, but why stop there? Travel over into the men's section and take a look. Not only will you find misfiled items (a woman's jacket mixed in with men's outerwear), but you can also find goodies that can be repurposed to suit your unique tastes. Here are four useful "not my department" haunts:

The children's section. If you are a women's size 8 or under, take time to skim the children's sweater and tops aisle. Hand-knit items from grandmas can be found, and a regular size child's T-shirt can work as an adult's crop top. Another plus: children grow out of clothing quickly, so finding barely worn items is common.

The lingerie and nightgown section. So many women are wearing slips and nightgowns as daywear that tony lingerie labels such as La Perla now offer daywear lines. You might not find many pricey La Perla slips, but the lingerie section can be a goldmine for vintage full slips, lace-filled peignoir sets not worn since the honeymoon, and interesting nightgowns that can double as evening wear.

and Etsy and quickly found vintage 1970s gray suede shoes from Italy that had cool square Puritan buckles from dustymillerantiques.etsy.com. They were $32, plus shipping.

✱ Put clothing and shoe sizes of family members in a notebook or on your smartphone so you'll always have them with you. A cloth measuring tape is useful, for checking sleeve lengths or inseams if tags are missing. (Don't know your sizes in those areas? Measure a pair of pants or

Men's dress shirt aisle. Some people who sew make paper patterns of their best-fitting blouses, thrift high quality men's dress shirts, and then use their patterns to cut the shirts down to their size. (See costume designer Rachel Apatoff's description and photos in chapter 7, "Clothing Rx.") Others make children's clothing from adult versions. (See Chelsea Confalone's remade infant and toddler wear in chapter 8, "From Plain to Pow.") No sewing ability? Wear the oversized men's shirts as is. The boyfriend shirt is a fashion trend that never goes away.

Men's coat aisle. Unfair but true: men's blazers and suit jackets have much better tailoring than women's. Cutting one down to size is a job to leave to a professional tailor, but the alteration charge is worth it when you run across a blazer made from a supple Italian wool in a pattern or tweed you would wear. And some of the smaller men's sizes fit women just fine.

Men's Raf Simons coat at a bargain price, $2 (Salvation Army), anchors a hi-lo outfit. Nora's tank is her own; Zara pants and necklace, each $2 (Salvation Army); Art Deco bracelet, $5 (S.F.V. Rescue Mission Super Thrift Store); BCBG Paris shoes, $6 (Salvation Army).

shirt you love and keep the measurements with you. If you are searching for children's clothes, bring a garment of theirs that fits for comparison.) If you are trying to match a particular color, carrying paint swatches is easier than dragging the clothing item with you on every trip. You frequently run into European size labels in clothing and shoes, so having a conversion chart on your smartphone or printed out in your purse will save you looking it up every time. Chapter 9, "Shopping Aids," has conversion charts that you can photograph to keep in your phone.

✳ The smartphone is your copilot while you are thrifting. Use it for on-the-spot research to check on brand names, jewelry maker's marks, and the like. It can help you identify those obscure designers that make your $5 purchase a $1,500 find.

✳ Pay particular attention to items hanging at the ends of racks and the returned items by the dressing rooms or checkout counter. These items sparked someone's interest, and although they did not make their cut, they may make yours. This maneuver is particularly useful on sale days. On those days, shoppers will often snag clothes quickly to beat the competition and take mountains of clothing into the fitting rooms, leaving some of the best pieces on the floor. Your best buy might be tied up in this fitting room limbo, so keep your eyes on what others leave behind.

✳ Prior to sale days, it's a sad fact that some people will hide women's clothing in the men's section so they have a better chance of buying them at a discount. We even found designer cashmere sweaters hidden under a pile of linens in an enclosed chest on a sale day. There are also more innocent times when people simply misplace clothing. Thrift stores are filled with misfiled items: men's dress shirts in with women's blouses, women's pants with men's slacks, sweaters in outerwear, silk nightgowns with evening dresses, and so forth. That tailored woman's blazer you are seeking just may be hanging amid the men's sport coats. The long-sleeved shirt section, in particular, seems to be a repository for all kinds of clothing that belongs elsewhere. The men's suit section often has long suit coats mixed in with sport coats. To tell the difference, look at the buttons. If it has blazer buttons, it's a sport coat. If you find a nice suit coat without the pants, go looking for them. They may be hanging in with the men's dress pants.

✳ If a favorite store takes in most of its donations on weekends, you may want to shop Mondays and Tuesdays, when employees have just priced and put out new items. Also on the days following a big sale,

THRIFT STORE LINGO

Resale shops have their own vocabulary. Some terms that are useful to know include

- **Closeout merchandise**—Goods that have been liquidated from retail stores, either because the style didn't sell or because the store was overstocked
- **Consignment contract**—A written document that both sellers and stores sign. It should specify the length of the consignment period, the percentage the seller and store receive, and what happens to unsold merchandise.
- **Dead stock**—New, unsold items that may still have original price tags but can be several seasons, or even decades, old
- **Discontinued garments**—Unsold items from manufacturers that are no longer making certain styles
- **eBay stores**—Used by many online resellers exclusively or as an add-on to an online store's own website. Features garments and accessories collected and photographed for sale by either an individual or a company, using eBay auctions or Buy It Now (BIN) sales
- **Good condition**—Normal wear; no stains, snags, missing buttons
- **Like new**—Close to perfect
- **Mint condition**—In pristine condition; as new

Abbreviations Used in Item Descriptions:
- **NWT**—New with tags
- **NWOT**—New without tags
- **NOS**—New old stock
- **NIB**—New in box
- **NR**—No reserve price (for auctions)
- **T** or **FR**—Italian size, French size

thrift stores can lack fresh merchandise until employees have time to start processing new goods.

✳Look at racks from several vantage points: from a distance, from different angles, and close up. Often racks are so stuffed with cloth-

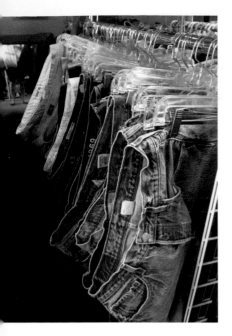

Pant waists hung outward so the sizes can be easily read is a real time-saver when shopping. *Photo/Allison Engel*

ing that finds can be wedged in between other garments. It is often on that step back that you can see something wonderful pop out at you.

✳ If you have an inkling of interest in a garment, keep it with you while you browse. So many times we have lost out on a good piece because we second-guessed ourselves, put it down, and someone else picked it up.

✳ If you spot a few items grouped together, like three long-sleeved cotton shirts that all appear to be freshly laundered and ironed, there's a good chance they are the same size and came from the same donor. Similarly, you can sometimes find several pairs of shoes in the same size and condition—again, likely from one donor. "The key is to be observant," says costume designer Angela Lampe. "Someone with great taste in your size may have

All these Enzo Angiolini leather shoes were the same size: a bonanza if it was your size, too. *Photo/Allison Engel*

WHAT THE PROS KNOW: HOW TO CONSIGN

Joyce Sobczyk, a former personal shopper at Bloomingdale's in Chicago, now lives in Florida, where she helps clients downsize their clothing collections. Because area consignment shops value her evaluation skills, honed from her earlier years with Neiman Marcus and Saks, she is able to bypass the usual limits on the number of garments that are permitted to be brought in per appointment.

Here are her tips for bringing in consignment-worthy items. Follow them and you'll avoid the embarrassment of having your clothes rejected.

- Items must be smoke free and from a pet-free home. No cat or dog hair. Not even the smallest snag.
- Most consignment shops require garments to come directly from the dry cleaners, on hangers in the plastic bag.
- The item must have a label.
- You'll have better odds consigning a top rather than pants. Stores have too many pants because customers don't want to try them on.
- Know whether the consignment shop is high-end (St. John, Chanel) or mainstream (Chico's, Liz Claiborne, Eddie Bauer) and don't try consigning mainstream to high-end shops.
- Clothes should be less than two years old, unless they are classic and somewhat timeless pieces. Designer vintage is the exception.

dumped their whole wardrobe when they lost weight. You may pick up all of it in one trip."

✱ Be aware that many shops regularly bring out new racks or carts filled with new items—sometimes announcing the arrival via a public address system.

✱ Dressing rooms, if available at all, are usually limited. So wear leggings and a close-fitting T-shirt or camisole so you can try items on

Better thrifts, like this airy Goodwill store, will have dressing rooms.

in the aisles. By wearing a cross-body purse you can avoid leaving your purse unattended while you are focused on how a garment fits. For men, wearing non-bulky items also helps. For both, wear slip-on shoes.

✱ Take size labels with a grain of salt. New clothing may not have sold for a common reason: the size label was incorrect. Sizes from different manufacturers vary widely, and you may want an oversized look or choose a small size to wear as a cropped top. What the designer may have envisioned as a mini dress may be an oversized blouse on someone else. Granted, the overall look may not be the designer's vision of what the item should look like, but once you pay for it, you get to decide how to wear it. Being divorced from the designer's vision actually lends itself to creative freedom. (A hint on size labels: In men's suit coats, the label is often hidden inside an inner breast pocket.)

✱ Treat some brand logos skeptically. Several international brands, such as Polo, lost their logo copyright, which allows knockoff companies to use the identical logo. The manufacturing by the imitators, obviously, is not as good, but their makers know that shoppers often seek prestige over quality.

✱ Also treat some clothing labels skeptically. Technology allows fake labels to be printed and embroidered with precision, so much so that there is a phrase for the practice: "ghost labels." And sometimes labels are cut out or defaced or—in the case of handmade items—were never there to begin with. Full-price stores sometimes remove or deface labels when they donate new items to thrift stores so thrift shoppers can't return the items to the full-price stores.

✱ If the shoe size is worn off the inside and not stamped on the sole, compare the shoe with another pair that has a clearly marked size. Also, since thrifted shoes are usually broken in, they may be bigger than the size listed. This may work in your favor if you stumble on a 9 ½ and you are a 10. Always bring a pair of socks, peds, or knee-high stockings to try on shoes.

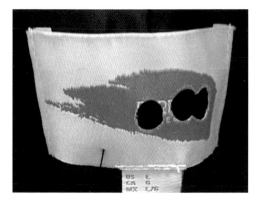
A label with the brand name punched out.

✱ It's often hard to tell how something will look when it's hanging on a hanger. Costume designers, who always are shopping for others, have been known to try something on a store mannequin to visualize how it will look on a person.

✱ Fast fashion means the fabrics will be thinner, the linings cheaper or nonexistent, the seams may be weaker, and the thread may be acrylic or plastic instead of cotton. Many fast fashion garments cannot be altered because there isn't enough fabric to let out seams. If you choose high fashion/low quality clothes, consider them as-is purchases.

✱ Sometimes unusual accessories are put in toy bins if store employees are unfamiliar with styles like Betsey Johnson's cat and lips purses, for example.

✱ Check all clothes carefully for wear and stains, but be particularly thorough in examining children's clothes. Children are rough on clothes, so stains as well as worn knees and elbows are common. However, children's special occasion items such as dresses and suits often look as if they never saw action.

✱ It's an obvious point, but the best prices will be on items that are indigenous to the area you are shopping, and thus more plentiful. You'll pay less for cowboy boots and shirts in the Southwest than in resale shops in Chicago, for example.

✱ Save your receipt. Goodwill, Salvation Army, and other stores allow exchanges, although rules have tightened in recent years. Gone are the days of cash refunds, and there often is a time limit on returns.

✱ Subscribe to a store's e-mail announcements. You get advance notifications of upcoming sales and discounts, some of which are not advertised. Stores regularly sell all clothes for $2 or $3 on certain days, and many have in-store specials on garments from certain

Daily promotions are common at thrift stores. *Photo/Allison Engel*

DIFFUSION LINES

Finding bargains at thrift stores is often a case of exploiting the difference between what the shop owners and employees don't know and what you do. Labels cause much of the mismatch in knowledge. While browsing a store's inventory, you may find instantly recognizable "designer" brands such as MICHAEL Michael Kors. This brand's items are marked up because Michael Kors is a sought-after label. But MICHAEL Michael Kors is a diffusion line and does not have the same quality or appeal as the original Michael Kors collection line. You can find MICHAEL at discount stores all day long.

Big names in the fashion business charge big prices for their collections. Collections will usually carry the full name of the designer and nothing else. If you find pieces labeled simply Ralph Lauren, Donna Karan, Giorgio Armani, or Dolce & Gabbana, you probably have stumbled onto a gem. When you run into labels that carry some variation of a designer's name, such as Lauren, DKNY, Emporio Armani, or D & G, you have come across a piece of diffusion line clothing. (See a list of diffusion brand names in chapter 9, "Shopping Aids.") Diffusion lines are more affordably priced and are aimed at the average consumer. They are usually higher quality than fast fashion and can be found at major department stores and discount retailers. Designer names can be an instant clue to high-end quality if the item is from the designer's couture collection. The quality of diffusion lines is more hit or miss.

To add to the confusion, some designers are dropping their diffusion lines (example A: Marc

FROM TOP: Donna Karan diffusion line; Ralph Lauren diffusion line; Emanuel Ungaro diffusion line.

continued

by Marc Jacobs) in favor of making short-term collections for major discount retail chains such as Target and H&M.

As Alec Leach wrote in a thoughtful column for *Highsnobiety*: "As the Internet has exposed people to everything the world has to offer at once, luxury houses with an expansive network of labels offering roughly the same product risk confusing—or worse, boring—a customer that has access to a dizzying array of fashion at their fingertips. Why waste time stumbling through Burberry, Burberry London, Burberry Sport, Burberry Brit and Burberry Prorsum when you could be getting to know the latest avant-garde Korean streetwear sensation or diving headfirst into the world of Scandinavian minimalism?" (Read his entire op-ed at highsnobiety.com/2015/04/09/diffusion-line.)

Isaac Mizrahi, one of the first guest designers for Target, was joined by Zac Posen, Misook, Rodarte and other high end designers.

Thrift store employees often confuse diffusion lines and designer lines for discount stores with designer collection lines. They may move the cheaper items into their "boutique" or "designer" sections at inflated prices well above what the clothes retailed for new. We've seen Simply Vera Vera Wang and Princess Vera Wang label dresses (diffusion lines created exclusively for the middle-of-the-road department store Kohl's) priced at $40 in a thrift store "boutique" section, when similar dresses in those current lines can be purchased new and on sale for half that at Kohl's. Similarly, items from the Missoni line produced a few years ago for Target regularly can be found with price tags suited for couture Missoni clothing.

High quality items and lower end trendy items can play well together. Mixing the two is called hi-lo dressing, and it is a badge of fashion honor to pull it off seamlessly. However, if you know your labels, you won't be paying top dollar at the thrift store for garments that should be priced with mid-level clothing.

If you are up on your labels and know off-the-beaten-path designer brands, you can take advantage of the fact that a more obscure name is likely to slip by those doing the pricing at thrift stores. For example, recently we came across a simple black scoop neck tee that was not in the resale shop's "boutique" section and had been placed in a rack of athletic and tourist T-shirts. The label was "Misook," which we knew is an expensive designer brand. The mint-condition tee that we bought for $5.99 is actually a $188 find. Not a bad day at the thrift shop.

departments. We are fans of "everything you can fit in a bag for $10" sales.

✱ Carry a small flashlight or use the press light on your phone or key-chain to check for moth holes.

✱ Keep a plastic bin in your car to quarantine thrifted clothes. Do not take natural fibers such as wool and cashmere from the thrift store to your closet. Dry-clean them first to ensure you do not introduce moths, moth eggs, or other insects into your wardrobe. Wash everything else before wearing. (See chapter 7, "Clothing Rx," for more about renewing secondhand finds.)

✱ Keep a bottle of hand sanitizer in your car or purse to clean up after flipping through racks. We've seen really dedicated thrifters walk around stores wearing knit gloves, the better to carry metal hangers for long periods of time without getting their fingers dirty.

✱ Final tip: If you are still flummoxed about how to start thrifting, there's the *ThriftStyle* never-fail Blazer Run. You start with a Little Black Something. It could be that queen of all perennial pieces, the little black dress (LBD), which you can find in all sizes and styles in thrift shops.

1

4

ABOVE: Yolander starts her blazer shopping with a one-piece black Vince pants suit, $8; and Me Too shoes, $6 (both Salvation Army).

(1) Mesmerize, $7.99 (Salvation Army); **(2)** Bazar Christian LaCroix, $6.99 (Salvation Army); **(3)** Evan Picone, $7.99 (Salvation Army); **(4)** J. Crew, $5.99 (Goodwill); **(5)** Unlabeled, $1 (Goodwill Outlet); **(6)** Don Loper Beverly Hills, $4.99 (Salvation Army)

2

3

5

6

7

(7) Donna Rae New York, $5.99 (Goodwill); **(8)** Monsoon, $9.99 (Goodwill); **(9)** Flores & Flores, $7.99 (American Way Thrift)

(10) Kenar, $5.99 (Goodwill); **(11)** Stephen Sprouse, $5.99 (Salvation Army); **(12)** Oscar de la Renta, $8.99 (Salvation Army).

10

8

9

11

12

WHAT'S IN A NAME?

The secondhand clothing market is made up of several different kinds of businesses. Some names are interchangeable, but there are some distinctions. Most of the venues below can be brick and mortar locations as well as web shops and mobile apps.

- **Thrift Store**—A retail store featuring secondhand items, mostly donated. Can be run by a charity, which typically does not pay for its inventory; or by a for-profit company, which may pay donors for items. Retail stores and manufacturers may donate new, unsold clothing for tax purposes. Online thrift stores may supply potential sellers with "clean your closet" bags and prepaid shipping labels as a convenient way to acquire goods. A thrift store may be a solo shop operated by a hospital auxiliary with quirky hours and a hard to find location, or a chain operation with dozens of outlets offering standard retail hours.

- **Consignment Shop**—A store, either actual or online, that sells items on behalf of the original owner, who receives a percentage of the selling price. Goods have to be vetted and accepted by the shop owners, who typically keep the merchandise on sale for only a set period of time. If unsold, the items are either retrieved by the original owner or donated to charity by the shop owners. Typically, brick and mortar shop owners set the price. Several online consignment shops let consigners photograph and price their goods, while others handle the photography and price setting themselves.

- **Resale Shop**—Any venue where used goods are sold.

- **Vintage Store**—A shop, either a physical location or online, that focuses on items that are at least twenty years old and, more typically, clothes and accessories dating to the decades from the 1930s to 1980s.

- **Auction House**—A firm that holds a competitive bidding process for selling clothes and accessories. Auctions are held either online, where you bid against a virtual audience, or in person, at homes, farms, businesses, or in regular or special events at the auction company's venue.

Organized thrift stores usually will color coordinate their items, so a LBD is easily found. The concept of building an outfit around a black base works even when it isn't a dress. In the preceding pages, we went with a little black one-piece pants suit. This suit is a well-made piece by Vince, and it was $8 at Salvation Army. On top of this, we added different styles of thrifted blazers to illustrate how a well-fitting piece of black clothing can anchor many looks and take you through every season. Blazers are usually our first stop in a thrift store because they make a fashion statement quickly, and quality ones are plentiful.

3

finding your style

Let's be truthful. One of the biggest barriers to thrifting is facing the big, bad mountain of stuff waiting in stores. It is nameless and shapeless, a daunting inventory that easily can make a person crazy. Many people walk into a thrift shop and are simply overwhelmed. Or, they get seduced by the low prices and buy armfuls of clothing they will never wear.

Beyond the tips for navigating the store, you need to focus on self-discovery. You have to get introspective and clear about what works for you and how you want to express yourself in the world. You have to tap into your creativity and boldly commit to expressing it by what you wear.

Thrifting is thriving because more and more people are committing to the idea of individual style. The idea of one ruling trend is out

A typical thrift shop interior, in Georgia. *Photo/Anna Phelan*

the door. Having your style in focus will provide the blinders necessary to narrow a thrift store to bite-sized bits that are easy to manage and digest. Then you will walk into a thrift store and, rather than chaos, you will *see* code. It's like Neo from *The Matrix*. The static and noise fall away and you are left with actionable clarity.

Thrifting is not shopping retail, so there will be no signposts—mood music, lighting, and clever displays—to reassure you that you are cool, the store is cool, and anything you purchase will be cool. You have fallen off the retail map into a wild clothing mash-up. You have to create your own style map by studying fashion, getting introspective about your clothing likes and dislikes, and trusting yourself.

THE STYLE MAP

Before stepping into a thrift store, you have to draw your own map to know where your "X" lies. "X" is whatever makes your heart sing. Thrifting is treasure hunting. Any pirate will tell you that you don't treasure hunt without a map. You have to know where "X" marks the spot.

Some of the most amazingly styled people are devotees of thrifting. They can be effortlessly chic or over-the-top dramatic, but one thing is a constant: they are true to their look. They have invested the time to discover what works for them and made it their mission to seek out those garments that flatter and reinforce their signature style. They are clear on their "X." With a signature style in mind, they are prepared to navigate the mishmash of humanity's style palette to clearly target what belongs to them. Once you define your "X," items will jump off the racks into your hands because you can categorize what you see instantaneously. This takes some homework on your part.

Homework is essential, because at most thrift stores you will be met with a world of infinite choices—all items and no map. So it is imperative that you become savvy enough to create your own signposts that can lead you to "X." Successful thrifting means picking up personally relevant, wearable, quality clothing. Luck favors those who come prepared.

BECOME A STUDENT OF FASHION

Paying attention to what is currently hitting the runways will help you shape and develop your own personal fashion choices.

The Internet was developed by the military for strategic use. True, but another excellent benefit of the digital network is bringing fashion to an audience far and wide. Fashion and the Internet are now inseparable. There are online editions of fashion magazines, you can watch runway shows from around the globe, and you can check out the street styles of individuals everywhere and share your own by uploading pictures.

Every reputable fashion magazine has its online counterpart. Regularly clicking on these sites is an easy way to develop an eye for fashion and keep tabs on trends and tastemakers. If you like things old school, pick up the print versions. It's fun to gather a few fashion-conscious friends and a bottle of wine and together page through what's the latest and greatest. Any way you do it, studying the ads and editorial content helps you develop opinions on what you like and why.

Pay attention to how elements are paired, be they colors, textures, or fit. It's obvious when designers mix the first two elements, but pairing a fitted top with a flowing pant—or vice versa—can be its own style point that goes in and out of fashion. Bookmark or create lists of looks you like. When you get tired of the expertly styled pages, travel over to the "street style" Internet sites that feature everyday folks getting their style on. Some popular sites are streetpeeper. com, chictopia.com, and sartorialist.com. Here, regular people from all over the world showcase what they are wearing, giving viewers global fashion trends—and trends in the making—at the click of a key. Look beyond trendsetters in the fashion capitals of New York, Paris, Milan, and Tokyo. Discover what individuals with style are wearing in Johannesburg, Rio, Hanoi, and elsewhere. Every corner of the world has a fashion scene and we are now privy to it.

Alan wears a thrifted version of a runway look: Crossroads sweater, $6.99; vest, $3.99; Lucky Brand blue jeans, $6.99; Thomas Dean shirt, $3 (all Goodwill); new silver buttons, $2.94; vintage Rooster tie (authors' own); web belt, $1, covered with silk tie, $1 (Central Thrift); Cole Haan sandals, $14.99 (Angel View Resale Store).

WHAT THE PROS KNOW: MICHELLE RAVEN

Department stores have free personal shoppers to increase sales and build brand loyalty, and also to offer a higher level of customer support. Why not thrift stores? That was the brilliant idea of Michelle Raven, thirty-four, a lifelong thrifter who got her start as a cashier at the Arc's Value Village Thrift Store in Minneapolis while in high school.

The Arc, which has five Minneapolis area stores benefitting the developmentally disabled, liked Raven's idea. The service, begun in 2011, is so popular that Raven now has three "guest" stylists who also do personal shopping. Still, clients can wait four to eight weeks to be seen. The stores have discovered that personal shopping clients spend $100 more per visit than do regular customers.

To begin, clients fill out a questionnaire online. Raven and the other stylists pull clothes from the store racks before the client's appointment, selecting items that might fit their individual needs.

An unforeseen benefit is that clients find new styles and looks they never considered, because the price is right for experimentation.

"Some people leave with a whole wardrobe of items they never would have picked for themselves," says Raven, whose own closet is 99 percent

If you are still developing your own style, there's nothing wrong with copying or adapting looks you see. Trying to re-create an outfit by thrift shopping is an inexpensive way to see if something that looks good in a fashion spread looks good on you. We tried it for our friend Alan, who saw a runway look he admired. Here's the runway look and the version we found at thrift stores for him.

Haute couture fashion shows—the actual invitation-only events whose tickets are fiercely coveted by fashionistas—are available online for anyone to watch. Yes, haute couture clothing often seems weird, irrelevant, and nothing that a real person would wear. But change your mind about it because it can help you start to develop a fashion sense.

Michelle Raven.

thrifted. Raven has a good eye and intuition about what will look good on another person. "I'm asked, 'How did you do this, you never even met me before?'

"The difference is, I'm not in your head, thinking about your body issues. Before most people pull an item off a rack, they're thinking about five reasons why it won't work for them. They won't even try it on."

But because an expert shopper has pulled a rack of possibilities for them, clients will try on unlikely items. "I urge them to keep an open mind," she says. "Try new styles."

Raven cites one client who dressed so conservatively that her husband said her style did not match her vivacious and fun character. "I pulled colors she never wore and did some mixing of patterns," Raven said. "She came alive."

Now the client comes in nearly every season. Most recently, Raven saw her wearing high-waisted bohemian ("boho") palazzo pants. "Her style is now living her truth," Raven notes. "She has unfolded before my eyes."

Haute couture is the high art of fashion. It is "out there" because it is a pure artistic expression of the designer's intentions. The late Alexander McQueen designed couture that you would never see anyone on the street wearing, except maybe that walking art exhibit, the heiress Daphne Guinness. For most people, an outfit with high heels that resemble lobsters probably won't work at the office—not even the annual holiday party. So why does couture count for the rest of us? It serves as inspiration for clothing's fit, color, and boldness. In these exaggerations of clothing we see the use of color and form and sheer chutzpah to make a fashion statement. Even if you bring that down to real world size, you will still be ahead of the fashion curve.

The Internet also is home to excellent fashion blogs that critique trends and designer collections and generally demystify what's new. A few of our favorites are *District of Chic*, *Two Stylish Kays*, *Vintage Vandalizm*, *Style Chic 360*, and *Fashion Hound*. (See more in chapter 11, "Resources for Thrifters.") On these sites, you can read conversations about designers, trends, and the upcoming season. Spring fashion is previewed in winter; fall and winter are previewed in summer. This can help you get a jump on the trends you should be looking out for while you thrift.

KNOW YOUR DESIGNERS

When you are doing fashion research not only are you studying the look of fashion, but you should also be taking note of the names behind it. Designers are proud artisans who usually sign every piece of their work via their labels. Knowing those names can make you a great treasure hunter because you will be able to identify when you have struck designer brand gold. Few things are more gratifying than when you have just scored a $1,500 jacket for $10. All three of us have done this plenty of times. There was the Chanel camel hair sweater with gold buttons that Reise got for $6 and the cream wool Saint Laurent tuxedo jacket with satin lapels she scored for $10. Allison found a Christian Dior silk jacket in jewel tone stripes for $12, and Manolo Blahnik shoes with multicolor leather bows in mint condition for $11. Margaret got lucky at Goodwill and snagged a gray wool and cashmere Burberry coat, lined in the familiar plaid, for $14.99. Those are moments when full-on happy dances are in order. ID'ing designers is a great reason to take your smartphone into the store so you can do on-the-go research. Not only will you be able to identify great bargains, but you will avoid buying mass market diffusion line clothing to which a designer has lent his or her name. (See chapter 2, "Navigating the Store," for more on diffusion lines.)

Online retailers that offer items from a variety of designers are one-stop sources for seeing what's kinda now, kinda wow in the fashion world. An excellent source for men's fashions is MR PORTER (mrporter.com), an online shop that includes editorial articles and interviews on fit, style, and design. Farfetch.com carries items from 358 boutiques worldwide with designer clothing for men and women, and also has interesting editorial content.

DISCOVER YOUR STYLE ICONS

A style icon is a person whose manner of dress perfectly sums up your personal style desires. He or she is a fashion muse of sorts and can be your grandmother, sister, or the man you see on the subway every day. Some well-known fashion icons are Jacqueline Kennedy, Iris Apfel, still inspiring in her nineties, and Jane Birkin, namesake

LEFT: Jackie Kennedy's style is classic and timeless *Photograph by Cecil Stoughton, White House. John F. Kennedy Presidential Library and Museum, Boston.* RIGHT: Steve McQueen's style is still hitting the runways today. *Wikimedia Commons*

WHAT THE PROS KNOW: REISE MOORE

One of the *ThriftStyle* authors, Reise Moore of Los Angeles, is a diehard thrifter who discovered her personal style through thrift shopping. What started out seven years ago as a reluctant trip to a thrift store has evolved to the point that today she prides herself on dressing head to toe every day in fabulous thrifted finds—including accessories.

Reise Moore. *Photo/ Courtesy of Mike Lyon Photography*

"Pre-thrift, I would have called my style . . . well, there was none, but everything was clean. Not as in clean lines, mind you, but as in 'These pants, shirt, dress, and skirt are clean, and I put them on today' kind of style. I discovered my personal style—a little bit chic, a little bit edgy—through the freedom I found in thrifting."

Shopping retail limited her, Moore said. "I didn't have the budget to splurge on unique statement pieces or accessories. There was no room for creativity in the process. Now I am able to find pieces that 'say something' and I like my clothes to say a lot. They need to be well-made, quality clothes that make a statement and make me smile or make me feel badass, depending on my mood.

"I often have to laugh at the irony. I spend way less than I used to on clothing, but I have never been so well clothed. Go figure, it's the gift of thrifting."

Beyond clothing herself, Moore says she discovered a real appreciation of fashion and the stories clothes tell. "Thrift stores are

for one of the most coveted handbags, the Hermès Birkin bag. For the guys, Steve McQueen was a much-copied celebrity decades ago, but his cool style still inspires.

Style icons don't need to be famous. Pay attention to people around you. People with style literally pop when they walk the streets because their clothes have something to say. Take note of how they pull their outfits together, and how they coordinate colors, texture, and fit.

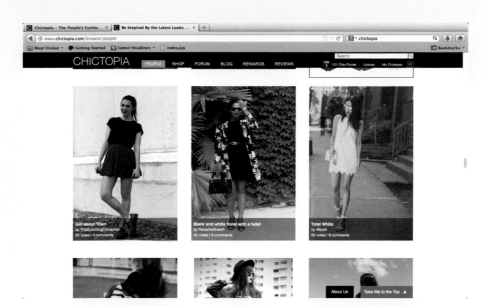

One of many "street style" blogs that celebrate individual style, including that of Reise Moore (CENTER).

truly fashion archives that evolve every day. I appreciate the inherent creativity of clothes: colors, textures, cut, buttons, zippers. The tone of clothes: innocent, sexy, hip, goth, country, urban. The seasonal reinvention and interpretation of clothes. The decade-based trends of clothes, from the twenties to today. And the history of clothes: What designer made this piece? When? Why? What were they inspired by?

"Thrifting turned me into a fashion geek, and I am proud of it."

DEVELOP YOUR EYE AND YOUR HAND

People who know clothing can simply glance at it and recognize the material it is made from. From years of paying attention to fashion or working in the industry, they have an eye for fabrics. You could also blindfold them and they would be able to identify a fabric by touch alone. They have a practiced eye and hand, and these two skills can

GUYS WHO THRIFT

All ages and genders are resale shoppers. Although women spend more time clothes shopping, thrift stores attract men who follow fashion and men who have a utilitarian view of clothes and don't believe in paying retail.

Brothers Brian and Robert Darrith grew up in Saint Simons Island, Georgia, and started thrifting as teenagers. Their high school Latin teacher clued them in to a stellar nearby store, the St. Vincent de Paul Thrift Shop in Brunswick, Georgia. Both Brian, thirty, a medical student, and Robert, thirty-four, a high school math teacher, have continued to be avid thrifters, finding high-quality bargains and treasured pieces of their wardrobes at resale shops.

Brian Darrith, in his $4 wool sport coat, outside the St. Vincent de Paul Thrift Shop in Brunswick, Georgia. *Photo/Anna Phelan*

"One of my favorite jackets, a red plaid, came from St. Vincent de Paul," Brian says. He has worn the festive wool sport coat, a $4 purchase, for Christmas gatherings and wedding rehearsal dinners.

He now lives in Savannah, and his brother now lives in New Orleans. When they returned home for the holidays recently, both made a beeline for their high-school thrift store. Among other finds, they scored with distinctive $1 ties and a red Boy Scout vest with patches.

Brian says he's a confirmed thrifter and not just because of the high cost of medical school. "It's the thrill of finding such great deals," he says.

knock a thrift store down to size very quickly. Knowing fabrics at ten paces, you can eyeball the racks and fine silks, cashmeres, and wools will jump out at you. You can learn to look for the telltale signs of quality clothing: bound buttonholes, full linings, boning, and more. (See chapter 6, "Clues to Quality.") With a practiced hand you can touch items and know instantly if they are worth taking the time to pull from the rack. If not, move on. When you do find that diamond in the rough, study it carefully so it becomes part of your fashion knowledge. Even if it's not your size or style and you have no intention of buying it, it's worth a minute to pluck these gems from the rack and study the elements that makes them quality finds.

SELF-STUDY

Label sizes in thrifted (and new) clothing are fluid. Not only are there different label-specific sizes—mostly owing to "vanity sizing," the practice of some companies attaching smaller size numbers to larger clothes—but also decade-specific sizes. The size 6 of the 1950s is more like a size 2 today. People are a lot bigger—taller and wider—than in previous decades. Add the different sizing metrics between countries and the listed size on a tag inside a piece of clothing begins to lose its primacy. What that means is you can ignore the numeral on the label as long as you are clear on what fits and flatters your body.

Give careful thought to:

- Where you like your skirt hemlines to fall?
- Where you like your pants hemlines to fall?
- Where you like your waistline to fall?
- What pants leg silhouettes are flattering and comfortable to you?
- Where you like your bustline to hit?
- What type of fabrics and textures are most pleasing to you?
- What season you are shopping for?
- What colors are speaking to you?

For example, if you know you are looking for a black wool pencil skirt that hits just below the knee and comes to your natural waistline, then you have just shrunk the enormous skirt section in a thrift store down to size. Your eye is going to be trained on what you want to find and you can literally walk the racks without stopping. For these types of specific searches we recommend building a clothing journal.

THE CLOTHING JOURNAL

A clothing journal serves as a "hit list" of items that you want to keep an eye out for at thrift stores. It may be that winter is coming and you are looking for that perfect bulky sweater, or you want to build a collection of cashmere sweaters. Put the hoped-for items in your journal and they will become the "X" you are searching for. Do this for every piece of clothing you see that inspires you. You can base your quest on fit, style, even color combinations.

One useful way of approaching thrifting is to hunt for "replenishment" items—duplicates of go-to items in your current wardrobe that may be nearing the end of their useful life. Thrift stores are excellent places to find a new-to-you version of your favorites, and possibly upgrade to a higher quality label. Keeping your shopping list to just these items can be another way to pare down a store's inventory to a manageable size.

On the other hand, thrifting is a great opportunity to purchase something that is completely

Misook leopard coat, $5.99 (Salvation Army); vintage Chic Debs styled by Norma Gale 1950s dress, $3 (Central Thrift); mother of pearl necklace, $5 (Salvation Army); Joey shoes, $8 (Village Cobbler).

out of your realm of experience. You can explore something new in fashion without a big financial commitment. For example, for a long time Reise wanted to love leopard print. It seems to come in season every year. But she could not pull off its boldness comfortably. One day she walked into the thrift store and found a beautiful Misook leopard coat. Because it was tagged at $5.99, she bought it. It was a chance that she could afford to take. That coat is now one of her favorite winter pieces that she pulls out of her closet frequently.

One of the allures of thrifting is the opportunity to explore the outer reaches of your creative expression without breaking the bank or skimping on quality. So go for it.

This speaks to one great big caveat to identifying your "X" and zeroing in on it: Keep an open mind. You are looking for that black pencil skirt and boom! out of nowhere a beautiful red silk skirt pops out at you. The hemline falls just in the right place, the skirt has a great waist, the quality is top-notch, and it's gorgeous. Even if it's out of season and not on your list, buy it anyway and put it away for spring. Because nothing is worse than walking away, having an item haunt your dreams, and rushing back to the store the next day only to find it gone forever. Thrifters have more than the occasional buyer's remorse. We have "non-bought regret," which you experience when you pass up something and miss the opportunity to own it. Remember that everything in a thrift store is usually one of a kind, so if something makes your heart go pitter-patter, it is most prudent to buy it, because you walk away at your own risk. The best thing that can happen with that red skirt is that you buy it and months later, when you are packing away your winter items and rolling out your springtime pieces, you are going to want to turn around and kiss yourself when you rediscover it. These moments are the best.

THE PSYCHOLOGY OF THRIFTING

Why buy a piece of thrift clothing? Joyce Sobczyk, a Florida-based organizer, works with clients whom others might call hoarders. She takes a more compassionate view and describes them as collectors.

She has seen all manner of clothes collections through her company, theclosetconsult.com, which offers home organization services and wardrobe styling. Her experience in sorting through clients' closets, storage units, and garages has given her rules about acquiring clothes. "One client had so much stuff in his garage, I had to get a Dumpster. Everyone's got too much stuff they can't get rid of. They can't let go."

Joyce Sobczyk.

She observes: "Many people are dealing with trauma, depression, or loss and shopping can be a release, especially if you're buying items for very low prices." She says shoppers should ask themselves these questions:

- Am I going to wear it? What's the occasion? ("I never buy on spec because when the time comes, I know I can buy what I need," Sobczyk says. "If you already own something like it, there's no need for another.")
- Why do I feel I need it? What am I going to get rid of to make room? ("I live in a house that's under nine hundred square feet, Sobczyk says. "I've learned when you bring something in, you must take something out.")
- Am I too disorganized to add more clothes to my life? ("If you're not an organized person, you have no right going to look for more.")

AVOID THE THRIFTING TRAP

Identifying "X" not only helps you find what you like; it will also keep you away from things that you *like* but will never wear in a million years. This discernment is just as important because the last thing you

The Grand Slam Golf polo shirt and khaki wool Jack Victor Prossimo pants, each $3 (Goodwill), fit Alan well, but they are not suited to his personal style. The runway look is.

want to do is spend money (even when you're paying thrift shop prices), invest in having the items cleaned and possibly tailored, only to find they are irrelevant and take up space in your closet. Thrift for quality and thrift for what you love, but, most important, thrift only what you will love wearing. Nothing is worse than a closet full of pieces dying a slow death. If you do have some slow-dying items cluttering your closet, donate them back to a charitable thrift store. Let them be someone else's find.

MOVE IN YOUR STYLE TRUTH

Personal style does not change from year to year. It evolves. It is not rocked by the latest trends nor does it change drastically from season to season. The most important thing is to operate within your style truth. The most iconic fashionistas are known for an effort-less, timeless, and unique personal style. This takes time to build. Dressing in your style truth helps shape your self-expression and confidence. Remember our friend Alan from earlier in this chapter, who found a look he liked on the runway and re-created it with thrift store finds? When he wore this outfit, he exuded confidence because he liked the style and the clothes fit him, both literally and stylistically. We thrifted another outfit for Alan that was also the right fit, size-wise, and featured quality clothing. But the style was all wrong for him. The polo shirt was not the tapered top he prefers, and the dress pants had front pleats—also not his style. The outfit wouldn't look out of place in most settings, but Alan felt out of place with it on. As you see here, dressing according to your style truth is about more than finding good quality clothing that fits.

Clothing must have the "X" factor that works for you. Style truth equals personal style equals the "X" you want to zero in on when thrifting.

Let the hunt begin.

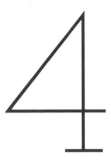

why vintage

What makes a piece of clothing vintage? There are purists who swear by the fifteen-year rule, those who favor the twenty-year rule, and those who pledge allegiance to the twenty-five-year rule. For the sake of getting us all on the same page, we are going to take the middle road. Let's say that vintage is a piece of clothing that was made more than twenty years ago.

Thrift stores can yield some great pieces. Although they are not stuffed with vintage finds as shoppers fondly recall from decades ago, it is rare that we don't find a coat or dress from the 1940s or 1950s hanging amid newer items. But be forewarned: Vintage clothing is a highly sought-after commodity, and in seeking out vintage you will be competing not only with other thrift shoppers, but also with professional resellers or pickers. These resellers are looking to supply inventory for

FROM LEFT: **(1)** Danielle's Donna Ricco dress recalls the 1950s, although it was made in a later decade: a testament to how some decades' iconic looks continue to inspire. Dress, $7.99; Fioni night heels, $8.99 (both Goodwill); purse, $3.99 (Salvation Army). **(2)** Mondrian color blocks were popular in the 1960s, and this later dress channels the look. Shoshanna, $7.99; Beverly Feldman shoes, $9.99 (both Goodwill). **(3)** Nothing says the 1970s more than the iconic Diane von Furstenberg wrap dress. Stacey wears a more recent version of that classic. Diane von Furstenberg Vintage, $7.99; black Nina strappy heels, $12.99 (both Goodwill). **(4)** This metallic knit set screams 1980s on Jordan. Contempo Casuals, $2; belt, $2 (both Salvation Army); Rock & Republic shoes, $24 (Clothes Mentor). **(5)** Costume designer Terry Salazar pulled this 1990s look together from entirely thrifted items. Tyler wears a vintage leather Xelement bomber jacket ($10), studded leather belt ($2.50) and bracelet ($2.50), and Doc Martens boots lined in plaid ($15) that echo the vintage Free People dress ($7). (Bracelets are from Melrose Trading Post; everything else is from Goodwill.)

50s 60s

online and brick-and-mortar vintage stores, high-end resale boutiques, and the international market.

Today's passion for vintage clothing, traditionally seen in Europe and America, is spreading to Asia, where past cultural disdain toward used clothing limited its appeal. Attitudes toward wearing someone else's clothing, especially if that someone has died, are changing. Style is overcoming superstition. Young women, in particular, are adding vintage to their wardrobes.

70s   80s   90s

Shops selling vintage handbags, shoes, clothing, and accessories are springing up in Singapore, Tokyo, Shanghai, and other Asian cities. They sell clothing from their own countries, as well as items imported from Europe and the United States.

Buyers worldwide realize that fine clothing, like wine, can get better with age, especially those iconic pieces that define different eras. We're talking about the bodice dresses of the 1950s, mod looks of the 1960s, chic wrap dresses of the 1970s, the body-conscious outfits of the 1980s, and the flannel and boots of the 1990s. These pieces speak to their time directly and influence fashion trends that are currently rolling out to market. It's no secret that designers regularly mine clothing styles from decades ago to build their contemporary lines.

Designers often make modern tweaks to the looks, such as slimmer leg widths or shorter sleeve lengths, as they seek to make the look their own in some way. But the saying "Everything old is new again" has never been more true than in the case of fashion. Think of the 1970s with its wide legged pants worn with snug fitting tops, its flowing light-as-air dresses or the androgynous "taken from the boys" pants suit look made famous by Bianca Jagger.

Designer Marc Jacobs is enamored with this decade, and his looks will often reference this period. The 1970s look has come and gone and come again in the last four and a half decades. The 1960s look has had its hippy, *Mad Men,* and Rat Pack revivals, and right now the 1990s grunge look with its flannel and oversized combat boots is making a comeback. Even the 1980s look, with its hefty shoulder pads and demure tie blouses, can be seen on current runways.

Shopkeeper Nicolas James Delgado of The Fine Art of Design in Palm Desert, CA, changes his window displays frequently. *Photo/Allison Engel*

High-end vintage clothing boutiques serve as archives where designers go to study clothing from years past to influence their collections today and tomorrow. If you don't want to scour thrift stores for a mint condition vintage piece, it is easy to find what you want in these treasure-filled boutiques. There is a substantial price markup, but when you factor in the time spent shopping to find a marvelous vintage piece in the wild, it is often well worth it.

One of the best-known, extensive (and expensive) vintage stores is Decades, a Los Angeles store opened in 1977 by Cameron Silver. He and co-owner Christos Garkinos stock

The Fine Art of Design in Palm Desert, California, has extraordinary vintage items in mint condition. *Photo/Allison Engel*

significant examples of twentieth- and twenty-first-century fashions. Their clothes often show up on entertainers from Lady Gaga to Rihanna to Jennifer Lopez, on the red carpet and awards shows.

Silver's book, *Decades: A Century of Fashion*, features the exquisite clothes his celebrated high-end consignment shop has acquired. But his store, while featuring the best from the past, has added digital technology to sell its wares. Its beautifully photographed items are available on its website (decadesinc.com), Instagram, eBay, and Facebook, as well as via trunk shows and from partners such as farfetch.com, featuring designer luxury goods for men and women. The store's blog includes features such as "Chanel Is the Fashion Lover's Hedge Fund," detailing how a 2006 Chanel jumbo flap bag that sold at retail for $1,795 has now tripled in value to $5,500.

Owners of designer dresses, shoes, and accessories from around the world ship items to Decades on consignment, and the shop will make house calls to acquire items in New York and Los Angeles. No longer

TALES FROM A VINTAGE RESELLER

Rachel Ericsen analyzes clothing for Dan May Estate Liquidation Services in Oakland, California, finding the right items that are valuable for resale, from high-end vintage to funky. This picky evaluator shares her knowledge.

On coats: "Turn the coat inside out and look for those with all seams underneath the lining."

On labels: "Vintage garments have tags sewn in, never printed in."

On unorthodox clothing: "Old T-shirts from rock concerts, motorcycle brands, and car-racing sell even if they're ripped and stained. The same thing with jeans. I found twenty pairs of one grandfather's Big 'E' Levis. Many were ripped and smelled like diesel. I sold them for $1,200 each on eBay."

On sweatshirts: "Old 1950s styles are big in Japan and sell for $50 and up. But the market is very specific. Our medium is their large."

On vintage's appeal: "In the 1980s, I wore punk clothing because I shopped in vintage stores. Instead of just being a poor kid who shopped secondhand, I had a cool identity."

On finding treasures: "The hunt is special to me. It's fun—a little bit of a thrill."

is there much secrecy or shame in selling one's former clothes. The store's website proclaims, "Shop Paula Abdul's Closet" and features a collection of her consignments, including Manolo Blahnik bamboo sandals for $260 and a maroon Gucci puff sleeve leather jacket for $945.

The store splits the payment fifty-fifty with consigners, although some Chanel pieces yield 60 percent for their former owners and 70 percent for Hermès accessories. The Melrose Avenue store has nearly five thousand consigners, supplying Decades with "neo-vintage" (from the last decade) to items dating to the 1930s.

Stores like Decades make vintage shopping easy, but there are still treasures and bargains hiding in thrift stores. We checked in with Pamela Jones, who used to own a 1950s vintage store in St. Louis. Now living in Florida, she uses her years of thrift store shopping experience to great advantage when making the rounds there.

"Anyone who knows vintage and brands knows Florida is a goldmine," she said. "People retire here and whole estates get given away to charity."

She notes that many resale shops have boutique racks in their stores for their better label merchandise. "Don't give up after the boutique racks because the people who decide often don't know," she says. "Keep going and you'll find good labels just mixed in on the regular racks." A recent haul by Jones included:

- Stuart Weitzman hemp and acrylic sandals, never worn, bought for $2.75 on "half-price Saturday" at the Punta Gorda Goodwill. Retail price: $200.
- Jelly version of Birkin Kelly handbags; one for $1.99, another for $3.99, bought at Consigning Woman, a resale shop in Punta Gorda. Currently selling for $85 on eBay.
- A Christian Dior light blue denim and leather handbag, with zippers and cotton lacing, in its original box with authentication certificate. Bought for $100 at Heritage Auctions, an online collectibles site. Retail price: $1,200.
- A Gucci camel-color woven handbag with bamboo clasp, bought for $85, also from Heritage Auctions. Retail price: $850.

Nothing is better than spotting retro trends on the runways and being able to rock an original piece from the era that nails the look. For example, if you are into "boho" and you are able to find and wear an original boho skirt from the 1960s, that is winning! Sometimes it may be that you find a great piece of vintage and while it fits the "look" of what is currently on trend, it is not the right cut. This is when you pull in your tailor to make it work for you. It's important to have a trustworthy team of clothing craftspeople in your life because you can take clothing to the next level by having it adjusted to your taste. Vintage purists may frown upon this advice, so you should proceed with care on alterations, especially on valuable pieces. Move down a hem or take in a side seam to make the clothing wearable, but don't alter fine vintage clothing beyond recognition. It would be like buying a pristine vintage car and putting 22-inch rims on it. No, no, no, and no. Modifications on vintage clothing should be done tastefully and with care.

Beyond the fact that vintage pieces can be worked into any modern woman's or man's wardrobe and lend a special dose of authenticity to a look, they are special because of their uniqueness. First, vintage clothing is a piece of history. When you stumble upon a garment by a renowned designer who made cloth-ing for celebrities or a designer who helped define the fashion of a decade—André Courrèges in the 1960s, Yves Saint Laurent in the 1970s, Stephen Sprouse in the 1980s—you start to realize that clothing can be something to be studied. You are looking at a piece of art history draped over a hanger, and it should be appreciated as such. Finding vintage pieces from designers such as Issey Miyake or Diane von Furstenberg is an opportunity to stop and appreciate their significance.

That appreciation extends to the qual-ity of the clothing. Watching someone who knows clothing inside and out (such as a cos-tume designer) take in a vintage piece of cloth-ing can be a real treat because they *get* it. They

This authentic Saint Laurent jacket from Paris was quite the find, $2 (Salvation Army). Nora wears it with her own blouse, a vintage pleated skirt, $8 (Myrtle Beach, SC thrift store); Ann Marino shoes, $17 (Collectors Corner); Ronay clutch, $3.99 (Salvation Army).

can feel the quality of the fabric, and they can see the craftsmanship in the construction. In a time when so much clothing is being mass-produced to serve wildly fleeting tastes and then basically self-destructs, shopping for vintage clothing invites one to slow down and take in the real beauty of clothing. If you score a great piece of vintage, what stands out is the pure "taste" of it. It is made from fabrics with a soft hand, and you see attention to detail in the craftsmanship: bound buttonholes, quality linings, handstitching, and so forth. (For more on specific clues to quality, see chapter 6, "Clues to Quality.")

TOP: Courrèges label at The Fine Art of Design. BOTTOM: An Issey Miyake jacket we found at Salvation Army for $6.99

One useful way to date vintage American clothing is by union labels, which were often sewn into side seams rather than at the collar. These labels serve as iconic monikers of American craftsmanship, but they also help pinpoint the era, as the labels changed through the decades.

Studying labels is not an exact science, but at least you know when you see this kind of label you have stumbled on a piece of vintage. Cornell University has a well researched website dedicated to the history of the International Ladies Garment Workers Union with more examples of its labels. ilgwu.ilr.cornell.edu/timeline/union-label-timeline

Garment care labels sewn inside clothing also help in determining provenance. The Federal Trade Commission started requiring these labels in 1971, so if you find a manufactured item missing one, the clothing most likely dates from before that year.

There are vintage sites and gurus on the Internet who can help

UNION LABEL
OF THE I.L.G.W.U.

RN 29257

The top label from the International Ladies Garment Workers Union, or ILGWU, was used before 1955, while the bottom label was used from 1974 to 1995. Labels courtesy of the Kheel Center ILGWU Collection, Cornell University Industrial and Labor Relations School.

clothing hunters identify pieces by tags (who knew "one size fits all" is a dead give-away for 1980s era clothing?), clothing cut, zippers, sizing, and so forth.

An easy tipoff to vintage is if there is a label from a store that is long out of business. In California, we perk up when we see an I. Magnin & Co. label from that late, lamented luxury department store based in San Francisco, or from Bullock's Wilshire, no longer in Los Angeles. All across the country, there are garments in thrift stores from the many other grand old family department stores that were swallowed up by national chains.

This interesting embroidered shirt, on our model Richard, has a tag that looks like it's from the 1950s from "Bidwell, Fine Apparel for Men" from Newport Beach, California. The Bidwell & Company store is no longer in business, and the shirt has no garment care label—two signs that it is vintage. We found it for $3 at Goodwill.

Samantha Davis, a longtime thrift evangelist who works as a consultant to eBay, has a useful site that gives tips

for recognizing vintage finds, sammydvintage.com. In it, she notes that before 1958, clothing sizes in America were not standardized. Sizes then were generally six sizes larger than modern sizes, so a vintage size 12 would fit the modern size 6. When clothing sizes changed again in 1984, the ratio changed to four sizes larger. So the modern size 6 would look for a size 10 in a 1980s vintage dress, Davis explains.

More of her tips can be found at sammydvintage.com.

Archivia Vintage Fashion & Textiles is the site of a blogger who compiled links to university and museum fashion references, as well as timelines and resources by era, archiviavintage.blogspot.com.

With the help of these sites and others, you can begin to identify vintage and build a collection.

Knowing how to wear vintage also is important. Wear a 1980s jean jacket and you can look cool. Wear a 1980s jean jacket with a peplum dress, headband, and leg warmers and you are headed to the annual Halloween party. Wearing vintage is often an exercise in less is more. To avoid looking like you are in costume, pair a single piece of vintage with neutrals or classic items.

And here is the essential irony of vintage: your age plays into what kind of vintage works best. Older women have to be careful when wearing vintage that they are creating a look and not

Richard wears a shirt from before the permanent-press days. The Vintage Fashion Guild has a very good label "Resource Guide," with photos, plus a wealth of other information and links, http://vintagefashionguild.org.

WHAT THE PROS KNOW: A PASSION FOR VINTAGE

As a boy, theater costume director Joe Salasovich got his first job cleaning the floor at the closest retail establishment to his home in Lorain, Ohio. It happened to be a vintage clothing shop called Jay-Mar. Geography became destiny.

"Across the street [from our home] was this shop with ridiculously beautiful vintage clothes," Salasovich recalled. "I'd get paid twenty-five cents to vacuum. This was the early 1980s. The second I got the theater bug, I started collecting clothes. I started in that store, but also estate sales, garage sales, church basements, everywhere."

He was seventeen years old when he began collecting. "I started by selecting items that were interesting to me or unusual in their design. I learned designers and searched out labels. I like Bill Blass, Dior, Geoffrey Beene. If something's over thirty years old, I snag it."

Now Salasovich shops for vintage clothes four to six times every month. Most of his purchases are for the extensive costume shop at Arena Stage in Washington, D.C., where he has worked for the last seventeen years. "This allows me a broad focus, not to be searching for the one item I need, but to be open to what's in that particular shop," he said. "I went to a thrift shop yesterday and found a huge cache of 1950s ties for $1 apiece. Some are particularly beautiful. I bought almost all of them."

When you're in a vintage shop and find one great piece, keep looking, he advises, because often there are many garments from the same donor. In his personal collection, Salasovich has dresses made by Pauline Trigère, Claire McCardell, Mary McFadden, and other design icons whose pieces are hard to find.

He advises hunters and pickers today to focus on couture clothing from the 1970s and 1980s. "That's what I'd keep my eye on. Some of the 1980s clothes that we thought were ridiculous, that people bought for jokes—the beaded pieces, the jackets with big shoulders—are highly collectible."

He notes that clothing from the 1960s and 1970s may last longer than earlier pieces because clothing manufacturers in those decades relied on polyester. "Pre-1960s, it was cotton and silk and they don't hold up as well."

continued

TOP, LEFT: Salasovich found this 1960s-era Adolph Blank cotton velvet coat, made in Paris, in 1999 in Washington, D.C. Six years later, he found the matching purse at a Maryland thrift store. "I couldn't believe it. It helps to have a good memory for what you already own." TOP, RIGHT: These beaded Mary McFadden tops both were found at Washington, D.C., thrift stores in near-perfect condition. CENTER, RIGHT: Elizabeth Arden, known primarily for her cosmetics empire, designed this pink floral dress and jacket, which Salasovich found in a Georgetown thrift store. "Washington is a gold mine because of all the diplomats and others who wear designer clothing." BOTTOM, LEFT: Joe Salasovich stands next to a vintage dress and short white jacket that his mother used to wear to their Lorain, Ohio, church. "Ask relatives," he counsels. "You never know what they might have hanging around in their closets." BOTTOM, RIGHT: Salasovich collected this red shirtdress because it's an early design by Gucci. *All photos/Margaret Engel*

Among his best scores was a Yves Saint Laurent Rive Gauche red studded leather jacket from the 1980s that he found for $19.95 in a Virginia thrift store. A beautifully made men's vest from the 1920s, never worn, is a prize purchase from that vintage store in Lorain where he got his collecting start.

Salasovich shops vintage wherever his travels take him—the farthest being London and Nicosia, Cyprus. While at the beach with his family in Wilmington, North Carolina, last summer, he was surprised at what he found. "The vintage there is remarkable. Truly, truly good."

Going through racks assessing vintage clothing is easier now because smartphones can instantly give you background on labels. But tagless clothing with interesting style lines shouldn't be over-looked. Salasovich's motto is, "Look for labels, but trust your instincts."

aging themselves into a bygone era. Twenty-somethings can wear just about anything and it has the gift of irony. Their outfits say, "I meant to do this," and "I am making a statement." While the look is a grab from the past, it comes off as fashion forward. There is a point, however, at a certain age, when you can reach back for vintage and it can suck you back in time with it. It doesn't come off as "I meant to do this," as much as "I've been stuck in a fashion rut for years." Does this mean older women can't wear vintage? Absolutely not. It means that they have to be careful to make sure that their vintage speaks to current trends or that their vintage selection is not a head-to-toe affair. Better to choose a timeless classic treasure that works for decades. Trench coats, sweater sets, sheath dresses, and vintage accessories come to mind.

Since we are now in a time where we are conditioned to pay very little for mass-produced clothes, we tend to complain that they don't make clothes like they used to. The truth is they do, but those clothes come with designer names and high price tags. It is these finely made clothes of today that will be the sought-after vintage pieces of tomorrow because they have the bones to last twenty years. Fast fashion—not so much.

accessories

When you see someone really rocking a look, it is oftentimes the accessories that put the outfit over the top—the expertly placed belt; the perfectly tossed, devil-may-care scarf; the phenomenal piece of one-of-a-kind jewelry—all those things help build and round out an outfit. However, accessories are the first things to be overlooked or compromised, especially when we are on a limited budget.

For those watching their money, a thrift store can be a godsend. There is no better place to look for jewelry, scarves, belts, and handbags at reasonable prices. Read: insanely cheap. For those who are not into wearing thrifted clothing and prefer to stick to retail, you still have friends in the thrift shop, and they are called "accessories." We cannot say often enough that some of the most beautiful jewelry and handbags we have seen have been secondhand finds. The photos in this chapter illustrate some of those fabulous pieces of jewelry, scarves, belts, and handbags that have come straight from the thrift shop.

JEWELRY

No matter your taste in jewelry—dainty, bold, silver, gold—there are pieces to covet every day at thrift stores. While you may never find precious metal or gemstones, there are plenty of collectible costume jewelry pieces that you can discover. It starts with knowing what to look for. Higher-end pieces are usually signed by the maker with what are called maker's marks. Discovering a maker's mark on a piece of jewelry is a thrill because with the help of the Internet and sites such as the "Researching Costume Jewelry" page of illusionjewels.com, which is a virtual encyclopedia on jewelry, you can discover the provenance of a piece.

A magnifying glass or jeweler's loupe comes in handy when you are trying to identify the tiny signatures or maker's marks on jewelry.

You can learn remarkable things when you start to look into what artisan created the jewelry, when it was made, what design era the maker was inspired by, how world events shaped the materials used, who artisans designed for, and what they went on to create. All of a sudden, you see the bigger picture and the significance of the jewelry in a historic context, and you realize you have a piece that is more than just a pretty trifle. It is a piece of art and possibly worth hundreds of dollars.

This is one of the reasons that collecting jewelry has become a major obsession for many. To bring the subject down to size, the photos in this chapter organize jewelry by types. What follows are items found within the last eight years at thrift stores and garage sales.

(1) LEFT: Current piece, $19.99. Has an extension so it can be a choker or longer; RIGHT: Necklace from the 1980s that hugs the neck; good with an open collar or turtleneck, $7.99 (both Goodwill). **(2)** LEFT: Glass and gold necklace from the 1980s, $3 (Salvation Army); RIGHT: Silver glass crystal necklace that's current (not vintage), $4.99 (Goodwill). **(3)** LEFT: Vintage silver necklace, $3 (Salvation Army); CENTER: Very well made bracelet from the 1950s with Art Deco styling—also looks like a car grille, $5 (San Fernando Valley Rescue Mission Super Thrift Store); RIGHT: Vintage Monet necklace, $6 (Salvation Army). **(4)** Four medallion style necklaces. FROM LEFT: Enameled necklace from the 1960s, $6 (Salvation Army); Gripoix piece believed to be genuine Chanel, with telltale imperfect glass bubbles and heavy weight (the catch has been replaced), $12 (Salvation Army); 1940s "mourning locket" that opens to hold a lock of hair from the deceased, $9.99 (Goodwill); J. Crew modern piece, unworn with $50 tag still on it, $5 (Salvation Army). **(5)** Vintage gold beaded necklace with a broken clasp when purchased, $10 (Goodwill).

(6) Mother of pearl bracelet and choker, purchased separately. Bracelet, $3, choker, $5 (Salvation Army). (7) Necklace has plastic "stones," which makes it light enough to wear, signed "Graziano" (possibly R. J. Grazioano), $5.99 (Goodwill). (8) Silver necklace with smoky rhinestones. It's a current piece, $4.99 (Goodwill). (9) A wood necklace from the 1970s, $5 (Salvation Army). (10) Very heavy necklace with individually knotted black beads. Has an "S"-clasp. Best guess: 1980s, $9.99 (Goodwill) (11) An example of two different purchases, but a close match that could be worn together. Blue bead necklace, signed "Monet," $2 (Salvation Army); blue clip earrings, $3 (Angel View Resale Store). (12) Black Austrian crystal necklace and bracelet, bought a week apart, $5 and $4 (Salvation Army). From the 1950s, because of clasp. (13) A bold necklace, $7 (Salvation Army). It is not real gold, which you can tell because the color is turning. Still a fun, show-stopping piece. (14) A hand ring, $4 (Salvation Army). (15) Gold cuff with a beaten exterior, $3; necklace, $3 (both Salvation Army). Probably from the 1970s when there were a lot of ethnic looks shown.

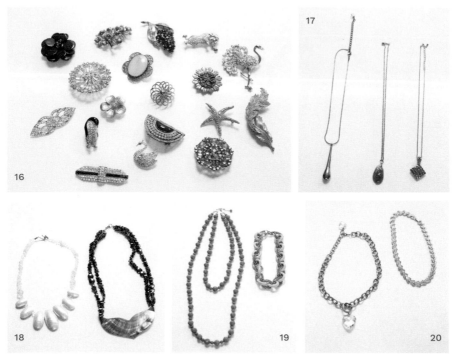

(16) A selection of thrifted brooches from Goodwill and Salvation Army. The Art Deco pin at bottom left with the blue stripe and the half moon brooch with the coral Inset were $4.99 each. The rhinestone flamingo at right is from the "ice period" of the 1940s when all white jewelry was the rage, $5. The white starburst at top left was the most expensive purchase, at $9.99. At center left is one of the oldest pieces, dated by the type of pin on the back, $2. The two leaf pins at top have cabochon cuts, not faceting, to bring out the light in the stones. **(17)** LEFT: Teardrop necklace, signed "RLM" (possibly Robert Lee Morris), $4; CENTER: Jade or imitation jade, $5; RIGHT: Filigree necklace, $2 (all Salvation Army). Real jade clinks on a glass, the color varies from light to dark, and it is cold to the touch. **(18)** Shell necklaces, probably tourist items, as they are artist made, not manufactured, found in a basket filled with similar necklaces, new with tags, $1 each (Goodwill). **(19)** LEFT: pink 1950s beaded piece with finished end caps, $3; RIGHT: Turquoise necklace, signed "KJL," for Kenneth Jay Lane, $6 (both Salvation Army). **(20)** LEFT: Current necklace, $5; RIGHT: Necklace from the 1980s or 1990s, $3 (both Salvation Army). **(21)** LEFT: Brown bead necklace, $2; CENTER: Gray and dark red beads, $8; Small beads and stone ducks, $5. (All Salvation Army).

(22) LEFT: Stone and bone and wood necklace and copper cuff, $1 each; TOP: Copper cuffs, $5 each; CENTER: Shells and metal bead necklace, $1; RIGHT: Polished wood bead necklace, $1 (all Salvation Army). (23) TOP: Vintage wood beads with a twist clasp and end caps, $5; BOTTOM: Wood beads and pendant necklace, $5 (both Salvation Army). Many wood pieces are from the 1940s when World War II made it difficult for jewelry manufacturers to get metal. Wood jewelry made a comeback in the 1970s as part of the ethnic look. (24) Vintage necklace, $5, originally priced at $15 (Salvation Army). Coral cabochon with seeded pearls has little owls on each side cap. (Cabochon is a style of gem cutting in which a gem or bead is cut in a polished convex form without facets.) Clasp is a shepherd's hook, which was used from 1930 to the 1950s until women lost too many necklaces. (25) TOP: Gold filigree beads and pearl necklace is vintage-inspired but a recent piece, $2 (Salvation Army); LEFT: 1980s power look necklace has hints of the 1960s, $4.99 (Goodwill); BOTTOM: Gold mesh bracelet with seeded pearls and a bar clasp, $3 (Goodwill); RIGHT: Very heavy freshwater pearl necklace, signed Barrera (possibly Jose & Maria jewelry makers), from a garage sale, $10.

WHAT THE PROS KNOW:
BARBARA BIGGS-LESTER ON COSTUME JEWELRY

Barbara Biggs-Lester.

Barbara Biggs-Lester calls it "checking her traps." This Los Angeles woman has been collecting high quality costume jewelry from thrift stores for the past eight years and has amassed an impressive collection of close to a thousand pieces. Her method is to visit four or five Goodwill and Salvation Army stores near her home and place of work on a regular basis. Most days, she visits at least one of the shops. By the end of a week, she tries to have made it to all her regular haunts.

Even if she doesn't buy anything, she says it is important to continually "check her traps" to help maintain her relationships with thrift shop employees. "They can't save things for me, but they'll point out new items that have come in," she said.

Biggs-Lester has become a self-taught expert on old jewelry. She has done it partly by visiting department stores that sell fine costume jewelry and examining pieces. "Go to Neiman Marcus, go to Nordstrom and look at better costume jewelry," she instructs. "You can touch it, feel it, see how heavy it is and turn it over and examine the back to see how it's put together. Then go to Forever 21 and see the details they take out to sell jewelry for $5.99. At thrift stores, you can pay $5 for Forever 21 jewelry or pay $5 for St. John. But if you know the names and know what makes them different, you'll make the better choice."

The other part of her education has come from collecting and reading dozens of books on jewelry making, jewelry history, and fashion. Naturally, she found these books—which fill an entire bookcase at her home—at thrift stores. Two of her favorites are *Fabulous Fakes: The History of Fantasy and Fashion Jewellery*, by Vivienne Becker; and *Collecting Costume Jewelry 101: Basics of Starting, Building and Upgrading*, by Julia C. Carroll.

Her library has come in handy plenty of times. A few years ago, her sister saw a necklace with a Chanel logo on it for $12 at a Salvation Army

continued

store and initially passed on it, thinking it was a knockoff because it didn't look like other Chanel pieces she had seen. When her sister described the necklace to her, Biggs-Lester looked it up and realized it was made with a glass called Gripoix, a colorful, imperfect, bubbly glass used by Chanel in its jewelry designs. Her sister immediately drove back and bought it. The piece didn't have the correct catch, so it may still not be authentic, but Biggs-Lester thinks the catch may have been replaced. "Don't discount an item simply because it has been repaired," she says. "If a previous owner was willing to spend money to repair the piece, it's a hint that it may be a high quality item."

Chanel Gripoix necklace, possibly authentic, $12 (Salvation Army).

Biggs-Lester says that thrifters shouldn't expect to find gold and diamonds at resale shops. Most stores sift out those valuables and sell them on their website or elsewhere. She has found silver items from time to time, as well as semiprecious stones.

"I wouldn't buy gold from anyone except a reputable jeweler," she says. "It could be gold foil or electroplated."

Precious gems and gold aren't the only jewelry items worth collecting. Good costume jewelry is highly collectible. "I never knew costume jewelry has the value it does," Biggs-Lester says. "Some people think the jewelry from the 1940s and 1950s is gaudy, but I love the artistry of it. They weren't dealing with diamonds and high quality stones, so they could let their imaginations go and made wonderful pieces."

Here are some other observations and tips from this veteran:

- Big, bold pieces are heavily represented at thrift stores. Biggs-Lester surmises that people receive them as gifts and donate them because bold jewelry isn't their style. If you are a fan of bold jewelry that makes a statement, "Start thrifting!" she says.
- In the early 2000s, everyone was looking for Bakelite, the early

plastic that has a warm, buttery color. Rub it and then sniff it—it has a chemical smell. It's rare, therefore, to find Bakelite bracelets in thrift stores. "Now, you are more likely to find Bakelite earrings than anything else," Biggs-Lester says.

- Jewelry fashions repeat, so if you are looking for 1960s Lucite, for example, be aware that Lucite came back as a trend two years ago. Wood jewelry was popular during World War II, when metals were scarce. In the 1970s, there was a revival of wood jewelry.

- If a piece of jewelry isn't real gold, it will turn color in reaction to air, chemicals in your skin, and perfume. Since such jewelry is worth taking care of, purchase a jewelry cleaning cloth to keep your jewelry clean and store it in an airtight jewelry case. If it isn't a highly collectible piece, Biggs-Lester recommends using spray shellac to protect the color. She stresses she would only do this with inexpensive pieces. There are detailed tutorials on YouTube.

- Purchase a jeweler's loupe or magnifying glass. They can help you to identify the teeny tiny signatures on jewelry and, if you know how to identify stones, they can help you discover semiprecious jewelry. Old school loupes range in price from $9 to $400. Of course, there is now a loup app: digital loupes and magnifying apps utilize the camera in smartphones to enlarge items.

- Types of clasps can be a tipoff to date a piece, although reproductions of antique clasps and "findings" (hooks, mounts, earring backs, etc.) are common and can confuse the issue. A vital online resource on jewelry identification is illusionjewels.com's web page "Researching Costume Jewelry." There you can find useful information on signatures and identifying your piece.

- Look for string, not plastic thread, between the beads of necklaces made of faux pearls or stone beads. When looking at a pearl necklace, look for pieces that are strung together and have a knot between the pearls. This small detail takes work and may identify a fabulous pearl necklace (which every woman should have). When you work with costume jewelry, the difference between a pedestrian piece and a great statement piece is in the

continued

details. Avoid faux pearls that have lost their luster. They are very expensive to repair and not worth it.

- Polished stones are cold to the touch and much heavier than plastic. Plastic "stones" are warm. Genuine stones make a distinct "clink" sound when placed on a glass showcase. If there is a pendant, make sure you turn it over and look at how the stones are fitted into the pendant base. Real stones are rarely glued to their base. They are more than likely held in place by prongs or fitted and encased in the pendant.

Biggs-Lester noticed that at the beginning of 2015, Goodwill started sending its better pieces from its stores to be sold on its website. So she has shifted her collecting strategy somewhat, adding more trips to garage sales. She has found that families often don't bother to individually price jewelry and will sell everything that's in a jewelry box or bag for one price. "You can get better deals because families are trying to offload a lot of fashion jewelry and just don't know what it's worth," she says. At a recent garage sale, she asked the proprietor if there was any jewelry and waited patiently until the woman brought out an entire jewelry box crammed with finds. "I bought 70 percent of the box for $25." Inside she found a pair of earrings that have become her favorites, by Polcini. (She is wearing them in her portrait.)

Biggs-Lester is wary of company-run estate sales because she has often seen companies cart the same non-bargain jewelry from sale to sale. She points out that there usually are not any bargains at company-run estate sales for the first few days. On the last day of the sales the company is willing to make deals. However, be ready to deal with crowds on the last day, and with crowds you may again see a rise in prices.

"I wear my jewelry—the sparkly stuff, whatever," she says. "You put on some basic clothing and make it your own with your jewelry. When people comment on your pieces, you can give them a brief history lesson. Next time they cannot wait to show you some of their stuff and learn about what they have.

"Some women put their jewelry away and save it for that special occasion that never comes, or the piece is forgotten. I feel bad for a never-worn piece of jewelry. I wear all my jewelry."

SCARVES

Scarves are a thrift store category that is easily overlooked. They don't take up a lot of space, so they are often tossed in a box or barrel in a corner or squeezed on a rack between the table linens and the comforters. If you cannot find them, make sure to ask a store sales associate where they are located.

Scarves are transformational fashion accessories. If you don't currently bother with scarves, once you buy a few, you will wonder why you didn't. They can take a little black dress or a neutral blazer and pants from so-so to wow in an instant. If you already wear scarves, you know that silk or fine wool scarves, especially from a top designer, can easily be priced in the hundreds of dollars. So finding an authentic Chanel scarf for $3 (which we have) is quite a steal.

It is also a good idea to keep an eye out for vintage handkerchiefs. They are highly collectible, especially the ones with maps or kitschy tourist designs. Don't confine them to your handbag or pocket. Use them as a pocket square or pin one to the front of a jacket. Expect to pay $2 to $5 each, except for at garage sales, where you can pick them up for as little as a dime.

Thrifting Scarves 101

Only buy scarves that are worth the investment of having them dry-cleaned, because the cleaning bill will usually be more than you spent on the scarf. For example, last week, we found several vintage silk scarves for $1 each in a bin among napkins, placemats, and other home textiles. The dry-cleaning charge was $6 each. They were still a bargain because these scarves, especially the vintage one signed "Vera," can easily be priced at $50 and above on collector sites. Hand-washing is an economy option, but make sure the detergent you use is specifically for delicates, such as Woolite. As with everything you thrift, check scarves thoroughly for stains and little holes. A competent dry cleaner

(1) Vintage scarves. (2) Knit and wool long scarves. (3) Knit and wool square scarves. (4) Vintage printed handkerchiefs. (5) Silk scarves.

usually can get out lipstick, foundation, and ink, but you want to be sure there are no longstanding stains that appear to be impossible to remove. An exception to this caveat would be vintage scarves. Some of these scarves may have a stubborn stain or small rip, but they have such a priceless cool factor—color, design—that they get a pass. Also, unlike most clothing with stains or flaws, scarves can be folded or knotted to cover up defects.

Designers usually sign their names right on the scarf, and the names are a mark of quality and their own kind of bling. If you ever find a Hermès scarf, you have just hit the scarf jackpot. Keep calm while you buy it and then cha-cha all the way home.

If there is no designer signature or label, look for quality natural fibers such as silk, cashmere, or lighter-than-air cotton, and quality finishing in hand-rolled and handstitched edges.

BELTS

The variety available in belts, especially for women, is tremendous. Skinny, gladiator, cinch—name a type of belt and a thrift store will usually have it. Women, especially those hunting plus-sizes, should not

(1) Wide belts. Bottom belt: WCM, New York, $3.99 (Goodwill). **(2)** Chanel gold link and leather belt, $2.99 (Salvation Army). **(3)** Wood and beaded belts. CENTER: Betty Belts, $1.99 (Salvation Army).

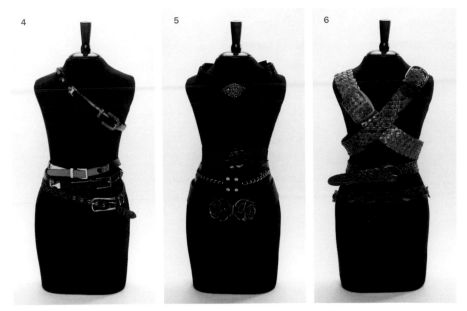

(4) Dress belts. Green belt, Mondi; red belt, Bally, both $1.99 (Salvation Army). (5) Cinch belts. TOP: Rhinestone belt, La Regale, $3.99; CENTER: Vintage red rose belt, Charmant Belts, $2.99 (both Salvation Army); brown rose belt, BCBG Max Azria, $6.99 (Goodwill). (6) Braided belts. TOP: Two from Linea Pelle Collection, $5.99 each (Goodwill); BOTTOM: Eddie Bauer, $2.50 (Desert Best Friend's Closet).

overlook the men's section for classic leather belts with simple buckles. Belts are also another opportunity to find some beautiful designer pieces. Well-made belts are usually signed on the inside and use top quality leather or exotic skins. They are usually heavy, because the hardware used is solid. The stitching is small and even throughout the entire belt, with no glue holding layers together.

HANDBAGS

Handbags are the BFFs of a woman's wardrobe. Reise Moore is the handbag collector in our trio, and some say she has too many. To which she replies, "How can you have too many when there are so many types and colors to be had?" She likes to call her handbag collection well diversified:

a collection for all occasions and seasons. It is also a collection that is fully thrifted.

Here are some of her tips on thrifting handbags:

✳ Stick to high quality bags that have supple leather, metal zippers, and heavy clasps, buckles, and pulls. The stitching should be evenly spaced. The lining should be substantial and well stitched. Non-leather bags, which represent an increasing percentage of the market, should have the same quality hardware, stitching, and lining.

(1) Perfectly structured. These iconic bags have inspired generation after generation of handbags: black genuine alligator; bone color Yokohama Takashimaya, both $3.99 (Salvation Army). (2) Two different styles of hobo bags: Black, Ann Taylor; green, Monsac embossed alligator, both $3.99 (Salvation Army). (3) These embroidered bags are highly collectible and often are pieces of art, $3.99 (both Salvation Army). (4) These oversized totes were a steal. The black bag is Bally and the red bag is made by French, a company better known for its luggage. Diehard Louis Vuitton collectors should be familiar with French, the company, as French's exemplary craftsmanship helped it land a license with Louis Vuitton in the 1970s to produce its handbags for the U.S. market. Black bag, $3.99; red bag, $12.99 (both Salvation Army).

✱ Always clean handbags thoroughly before using. Women live out of their handbags, so you want to make sure the last tenant has vacated the premises. Disinfectant wipes work well for this purpose.

✱ Make sure handbags are strong enough to survive another go with you. They've had a first life and possibly years of use, so check the seams and hardware for signs of wear, especially the straps and zippers. Most

(5) Beaded bags are sometimes handmade. White bag with gold chain strap, $3.99; Joe Joe wristlet handbag made of mother of pearl and beads, $3.99; Butterfly, $10; (all Salvation Army). (6) This saddlebag is a classic. It harkens back to the bags that were tossed on pack animals to carry goods. Lucky Brand, $3.99 (Salvation Army). (7) Patent leather comes in more than black. These handbags are vintage and give any current bag a run for its money. Pink, top handle; black bag, Bags by Francois California; yellow bag with canvas sides, all $3.99 (Salvation Army). (8) A fresh take on the classic quilted handbag. Diane Gilman, $5.99 (Goodwill).

elements can be repaired or replaced at a skilled shoe repair shop, but you need to do the math and see if your bargain bag is worth the repair bill.

✱ Signed bags are a plus. If an artisan has placed his or her name on the bag it is usually a sign of quality. It is also a good way to research the bag to determine value.

(9) Whiting & Davis was established outside of Boston in 1876 and is known for its metal mesh handbags. The company continues to turn out exquisite handbags and jewelry today. White tote with tortoise handle, $14.99 (Goodwill). **(10)** Metal mesh bag collection. Red and white bags, Whiting & Davis; black bag and white clutch, Whiting & Davis inspired, all $3.99 (Salvation Army). **(11)** This Calvin Klein suede duffle bag is fairly simple, but the hardware adds a bit of toughness, $9.99 (Goodwill). **(12)** Reise's all-time favorite handbag, a true stunner. Lewis, $8.99 (Goodwill).

(13) This small clutch is an elegant piece made by Gucci. It is not unusual to find high-end designer brands at thrift stores. We have seen Chanel, Louis Vuitton, Tod's, Chloé, and so forth. However, if you do not know how to authenticate them, you may end up with a fake, which is not worth the price at any cost, $3.99 (Salvation Army). **(14)** There are some bags that look beat-up and lived in, so you don't want to restore them because they have an outstanding patina, which is a good thing if you are going for the aged, lived-in look. This bag is perfectly weathered, j. jill, $7.99 (Goodwill). **(15)** This handstitched unstructured patchwork Johnny Farah tote is made out of fine suede and pony hair, $13.99 (Goodwill). **(16)** These handbags are all genuine exotic skin bags—snakeskin, crocodile, and lizard. Crocodile is a highly imitated print that is usually embossed on cow leather. Genuine crocodile will have a "dimple" on each scale from sensory hairs that were embedded there. Blue and red snakeskin, Leslie Hamel Atelier, $3.99 (Salvation Army); tan lizard, $9.99 (Salvation Army); brown lizard, Bellestone, $12.99 (Salvation Army); pink crocodile, Carlos Falchi, $6.99 (Goodwill); burgundy crocodile, $3.99 (Salvation Army).

(17) These totes are also called "shopper bags." They are lined in canvas and are the elegant workhorses of a handbag collection. Blue, Tod's; tan, Francesco Biasia, both $3.99 (Salvation Army). (18) These woven bags are a summer staple, $3.99 (Salvation Army). (19) This wristlet is a unique evening bag. Victor Costa, $8 (Salvation Army). (20) This bag is a one-of-a-kind piece. Woven with a Lucite closure, gold hardware, and a leather strap, Rodo, $7.99 (Goodwill). (21) This tapestry clutch had the original satin coin purse and mirror neatly tucked into the side pocket, Ungár, $12 (Salvation Army). (22) Crossbody bags are a summer necessity. They can be found in kicky colors and textures. Black, Ganson; pink, Carmem; tan, Loewe (unauthenticated), all $3.99 (Salvation Army). (23) These classic bags are closet staples. Guy Laroche, $8.99 (Goodwill); Bally, $3.99 (Salvation Army).

(24) These one-of-a-kind bags are their own conversation pieces. The half-moon marble bag looks like it has been carved out of the side of a mountain, but it is actually a piece of patent leather. If you are someone who craves unorthodox looks, the thrift store is the place to check first. The reason? People who buy or are given bold statement purses, like bold jewelry, may be uncomfortable with them, making the handbags likely donations. Tiger bag; Marlene's of Encino marbled patent leather; black and white Angela Frascone wristlet, all $3.99 (Salvation Army). (25) Bucket bags: Brown leather, Cristina; red leather, Bottega Veneta; handwoven woolen bag, EM May; jean and crocodile trim, all $3.99 (all Salvation Army) (26) Gold and silver bags add pop to any outfit. Gold handbag, Bulga, $3.99 (Salvation Army); silver handbag, Ganson, $5.99 (Goodwill); gold clutch, Rappi, $3.99 (Salvation Army). (27) Adding a pop of print—leopard or houndstooth—can be easy if you have the right bag. Houndstooth, Topkapi; leopard, Mary Kay, both $3.99 (Salvation Army). (28) This Vera Bradley handbag is a fun way to add some punch to a summer outfit, $3.99 (Salvation Army).

Thrifting accessories is an opportunity to just have fun with your wardrobe and experiment with new looks. If an item falls outside of the quality box but makes you do a little happy dance on the inside, run with it because more than likely, it will not be breaking the bank. Give it a wardrobe tryout, and if it becomes part of your style, you can always be on the lookout for a better version.

SHOES

Shoes! Thrift stores have shoes and, yes, some of them can be sketchy, hygiene-wise and wear-wise. Pass those up. We regularly find high quality shoes that are new, barely worn, or just need a new heel or a good shine. (See chapter 7, "Clothing Rx," for advice on what flaws are worth fixing.) We often come across designer brands such as Ferragamo, Gucci, Etienne Aigner, Marc Jacobs, and Manolo Blahnik, to namecheck a few.

One of our more startling buys was a pair of size 13 Beatle boots, made by Mark Astbury from Liverpool, England. They had barely

RIGHT: The Beatle boots are lined in red and have a side zip, $19.99 (Salvation Army). **ABOVE:** Our proof that the boots were authentic.

TOP, LEFT: A selection of men's shoes and boots we thrifted. All were less than $20 except the vintage suede Italian shoes with the Pilgrim buckle, which we ordered on Etsy for $32. TOP, RIGHT: Well-priced, barely worn women's boots and booties are not hard to find at thrift stores. The red cowboy boots were the most expensive of this trio, at $34.99 (Angel View Resale Stores). BOTTOM, LEFT: Thrifting is useful for those times when you want to take a flyer on something that might be a style stretch, such as over-the-knee boots. If you don't end up liking them, no harm, no foul. Purple boots, $20 (It's a Bargain); black suede Kelsi Dagger boots, $8 (Salvation Army). BOTTOM, RIGHT: Our wheel of shoe fortune includes red patent leather Ferragamo flats and Bally loafers, Bruno Magli heels, Manolo Blahnik mules, Beverly Feldman pumps, and Isaac Mizrahi Mary Janes. Prices ranged from $1.50 to $20.

been worn and were a cool $19.99 at Salvation Army. Googling this particular boot, we found a used pair advertised for $235 on eBay.

Reputable thrift stores will evaluate shoes before they hit the floor and only put out pairs that are customer friendly, which means clean and not overly abused. We do suggest an extra layer of precaution: disinfect your shoes. If you have ever gone to a bowling alley or a skating rink, you know there are shoe disinfectants that can help. Some shoppers spray the inside of thrifted shoes with Lysol. Shoe repair professionals often sell a deodorizing spray called Sneaker Fresh. Rocket Pure Natural Foot and Shoe Deodorizer and Dr. Scholl's Odor-X are other popular brands. Or sprinkle baking powder inside the soles and let it absorb odors for a few days before discarding the powder.

Leather can become brittle and crack over time, so look for shoes made of top quality leather that is still supple and can withstand the force of someone walking in it. Check the inside of the shoe and make sure the insoles are still flexible and comfortable, as they can become stiff with age and crack under use. New insoles, however, are an easy fix (more on that in chapter 7, "Clothing Rx").

clues to quality

When you buy thrift clothing, quality should be at the top of your barometer. Why? Because this clothing has had a life. And how long you will get to wear and enjoy the clothing depends on how well it was constructed and cared for. High quality clothing is built to withstand the rigors of wearing and laundering. That means the seams are strong and reinforced. The fabric is tightly woven. The buttons are made from durable materials.

When you buy clothing with quality labels you can be fairly safe in assuming that the fine piece of clothing was properly cared for by the previous owner. Since you will need to invest in cleaning the item, you want to make sure your dry-cleaning bill is not more than the item is worth. You are making an investment, even if the initial thrift store price is a bargain. Here's an example of the math. Reise Moore, being a sucker for stripes, thrifted an Akris Punto black-and-white striped 100 percent wool jacket for $8. It needed to be dry-cleaned, adding $13 to the tab, and had a moth hole in it, prompting a $40 reweaving bill. But it was worth the investments because after five years of wear, it still is a mainstay of her wardrobe. It is a quality piece of clothing, built to last.

Fast fashion has a tendency to fall apart. It is not meant to last season to season. It is designed to keep you following the trends and buying. If you are working on building your style, you want pieces that serve as sturdy building blocks. This doesn't mean you shouldn't get your fast fashion fix from time to time. But buy the fast fashion at the retail store so you can take advantage of its low prices—which are often comparable to what you pay for the same item at a thrift store—and take full advantage of its limited wear-and-tear lifespan.

This is why it is important to know your fast fashion labels and avoid them while thrifting. You don't want to fill your closet with poorly made clothing.

If you don't know labels, or if you come across an unfamiliar one, there are plenty of clues to confirm whether or not the garment on the hanger is a well-made, quality item.

First and foremost check the fiber content. Unless the interior content tags have been removed, you can quickly see what the garment is made of. When you see any of the following words, your pulse should quicken:

Alpaca—Made from llama hair

Angora—Made from rabbit hair

Camel hair—The real deal does indeed come from the undercoat of a camel, but over the years, it has become a generic term to describe tan coats. Check the label—a tan wool coat can have the iconic camel hair coat style and not contain a shred of camel hair.

Cashmere—made from goat hair, even softer than wool

Mohair—Also made from goat hair, often used in sweaters

Silk—There are a multitude of weights and varieties of silk, but labels don't tell you whether it is crepe de chine (lightweight and matte finish), dupioni (one of several silks with slubs), taffeta (known for its iridescent sheen), or any of the many other types of silk. And, to confuse the issue, silk is also widely used in blends. A silk-wool blend can be a more desirable, luxurious fabric than a 100 percent silk with a poor finish and stiff "hand."

Vicuña—A rare and expensive fabric

On Nora: Camel hair coat, $9.99 (Salvation Army); Adrienne Vittadini sweater, $3 (Central Thrift); handmade wool skirt, $2 (Central Thrift); Ecco suede low heels, $5 (The SonShine Shop); Loewe unauthenticated purse, $3.99 (Salvation Army).

with a soft nap made from a llama-like animal and usually blended with wool

Pure Virgin Wool and Wools with "S-numbers" or "Super S-numbers"— Pure virgin wool means that the fabric has not been recycled. S-numbers refer to the thickness of the wool fibers. The higher numbers mean a thinner, finer fiber and a more expensive fabric. Tags on men's suit coats aren't shy about touting their S-numbers. "Super 110" or "Super 120" will be in large letters. The highest S-numbers, such as 150, are usually found only in custom-made suits because the fabric is so thin it can be a challenge to work with.

These are examples of luxury fabrics, but it is important not to disdain the other types of fabric. For example, many people shun polyester due to the bad rap it got from the original polyester double knits that didn't wrinkle and lasted forever. Unfortunately, they were forever linked with bad pants suits. Now polyester comes in many different styles, weights, and hands—or how a fabric feels when you hold it. Keep in mind that Emilio Pucci designed iconic bold print dresses from polyester in the 1960s that are now highly collectible and worth thousands of dollars.

Although natural fibers are held in esteem, designers will use whatever fabric they think will best create the look they are trying to achieve. So make sure that you don't become so much of a fabric snob that you walk away from a masterpiece.

It's hard to generalize about fabrics, because there are hundreds of varieties. Fabric knowledge, which depends as much on feeling fabrics as it does on studying photos or videos, is gained after years of experience.

Taking research trips to a well-stocked fabric store can be useful, but there aren't as many of those around as there were during the boom

WHAT THE PROS KNOW: GREG LAVOI

At thrift stores, Hollywood TV and film costume designer Greg LaVoi goes straight for the cashmere. He doesn't let moth holes deter him, because he has a good relationship with a reweaving firm, and he knows that cashmere can be repaired to pristine condition.

His first purchase was eleven years ago on eBay, where he spied a secondhand black cashmere topcoat from the Neusteter Co., a defunct Denver-based department store that had a store in Colorado Springs, where he grew up. The store "was my Neiman Marcus," he recalls. It influenced him when he was a youngster and interested in fashion. The coat was $29 and arrived without any need of repair. He wears it to this day.

Greg LaVoi. *Photo/Erica Dorsey*

(This label nostalgia is common among thrifters. Two of the authors admit to immediate warm feelings for any item with a label from Halle Brothers or Higbee's, department stores from our youth in Cleveland, or from the Younkers French Room in Des Moines, Iowa, the city where we started our newspaper careers.)

LaVoi continued his cashmere overcoat collecting with "a fantastic 1950s taupe" found at a thrift store in Venice and a camel hair coat from one of the American Vintage stores in Los Angeles. On these, however, "the moths had a buffet," and both required reweaving. In later thrift

years of home sewing in the 1950s and 1960s, when every small town had a fabric shop. Large fabric chains—with their heavy reliance on inexpensive man-made fabrics—are now the go-to source for the sewing needs of much of America.

If you are lucky enough to live in a city with a well-stocked fabric store outings, he found a navy coat, and a coat identical to his camel hair coat but in black.

Cashmere sweaters were his next purchases, and over the years he bought twenty to twenty-five of them—V-necks, turtlenecks, mock turtlenecks, cardigans—most priced in the $5 to $15 range. Even if the reweaving charge pushed a sweater's cost to $100, LaVoi says the purchases made economic sense. "Cashmere lasts forever if you take care of it."

He almost never dry-cleans his cashmere sweaters, preferring to wash them by machine on a lingerie setting using Woolite. He either towel dries them or puts them in the dryer. Cashmere is very forgiving, he notes.

LaVoi, who also has designed a couture line devoted to the brilliant fashions of the late clothing designer Irene Lentz ("Irene by Greg LaVoi"), now looks mainly for international designer labels when he is in thrift stores. He recently found a white Issey Miyake shirt at a Salvation Army in Torrance for $2.50, as well as a few shirts from the British designer Paul Smith ($5) and the American Brooks Brothers brand (also $5). "I take them to my good cleaners and have them work on the yellowing, starch them up, and they're fine," he says.

For his Hollywood work (*Major Crimes, The Closer,* and many others) he loves to shop thrift stores, but often he can't because actors usually need to have multiples of each item of clothing. But when a character doesn't need multiples, he frequently heads to the nearest thrift. There, unlike most shoppers, he searches for less-than-perfect garments that show some wear. Says LaVoi: "The clothes there make it look so real, like the character has owned them forever."

store, patronize it. And when you travel, seek out fabric meccas such as the Garment District in New York City and the Fabric District (part of the larger Fashion District) in Los Angeles. Manhattan is the home of Mood Fabrics (it also has a branch in Los Angeles), which Tim Gunn of *Project Runway* calls "the Library of Congress of textiles." In 2015 Mood published an excellent source book on fabrics, *The Mood Guide to Fabric and Fashion,* which has clear descriptions and compelling photos of fabrics and how they are used in fashion.

In Los Angeles, there's no better place to buy (and learn about) wool and men's suiting materials than the venerable B. Black & Sons in the downtown Fabric District, in business since 1922. When in San Francisco, a must is a stop at Britex Fabrics, off Union Square, with four floors of fabric fabulousness. Britex has a longstanding swatch service, useful for finding a fabric to match a garment you already have. The company will send swatches of its online fabrics for $1 per swatch, plus shipping.

Happily, Mood, B. Black & Sons, Britex, and other quality fabric sellers all offer their wide inventories by mail, so anyone can have long-distance access to quality fabrics. (See chapter 11, "Resources for Thrifters.")

Charlotte Stratton, who teaches costume construction at the USC School of Dramatic Arts.

If you are buying quality thrifted garments, it's handy to know where to find top-notch fabrics, should you need to match or patch.

After searching for quality fabrics, study up on the construction details that show that extra time and care were put into a garment. Charlotte Stratton, who teaches costume construction at the University of Southern California's School of Dramatic Arts, and has spent decades examining purchased clothing and building original items, notes that manufacturers can skimp on one detail and add in quality on another, which makes it hard to pinpoint one feature that telegraphs quality. "So many decisions go into costing out how a garment is made," she says.

Still, there are some details that tend to be found primarily in better clothing. Give an item extra consideration if you see any of these features:

Pick stitching, as seen from the inside of a jacket.

Handsewn, tiny "pick stitching" on suit jacket lapel—These stitches hold the edges crisp and keep the underside from rolling up to the front. Alteration shops sometimes get requests to add pick stitching to a finished coat or jacket so it looks like a high-end garment. Cheaper jackets will have machine stitching.

Bound buttonholes—Making a bound buttonhole requires several extra steps. These buttonholes are so named because there is no visible stitching around the buttonhole, because it is "bound" by fabric. Bound buttonholes add labor cost to

Unusual vertical variation on bound buttonholes in a $3 thrifted blazer.

ANATOMY OF A JACKET

Men's suit coats typically have better tailoring than women's, although many of the principles are the same. We gave Charlotte Stratton, who teaches costume construction at the USC School of Dramatic Arts, two dozen thrifted men's suit coats of varying quality and asked her to show us the difference between them.

(1) The jackets were examined and tagged by Charlotte Stratton for telltale quality details. (2) A nice touch on this side vent jacket is a band that keeps the vents from flapping open. (3) This jacket, made with Super 120 wool, has an excellent interior finish. (4) A high-end jacket, but still considered ready-to-wear. It is fully lined and has pick stitching and interior welt pockets. (5) A half lining does not necessarily mean a cheaper jacket. This Alan Flusser jacket is a summer weight (55 percent linen, 45 percent rayon) and has a half lining to cut down on weight. All the interior seams must then be bound, adding to the cost.

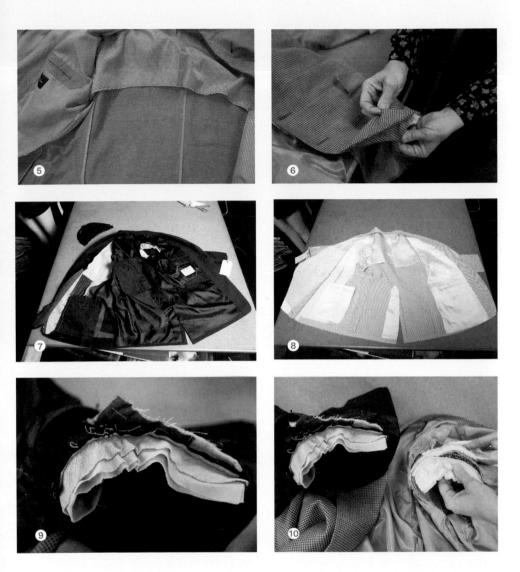

(6) Pinch a suit front near the hem. If you can feel three separate layers—the fashion fabric, the lining, and a separate layer of hair canvas interfacing—it's a better quality jacket. (7) The light gray hair canvas at left goes all the way to the hem–a "fully canvassed" jacket. (8) This seersucker suit has fusible interfacing, not hair canvas—a cheaper and inferior construction. (9) This jacket has a hand cut multilayered sleeve head, or facing, that fills the gap between the arm and sleeve top. (10) The jacket on the right has a ready-made sleeve head—sometimes called a "mustache" because of its shape—made of thicker fabric, for use in heavier suits.

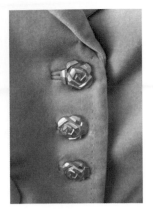

RIGHT: Bound buttonhole in a $5.99 thrift store blazer. LEFT: Bound buttonholes with fancy buttons.

a garment and are a tipoff to quality. A gray jacket we found for $3 had even more elaborate vertical bound buttonholes, with a fabric tab covering the button when closed.

Hand-worked buttonholes— Machines can mimic a handstitched buttonhole so effectively that they can be hard to spot. Turn the buttonhole over and look for imperfections in the buttonhole stitches, which are a hint that they were hand done.

TOP, LEFT: Hand-worked buttonholes as seen from the front. BOTTOM, LEFT: Hand-worked buttonholes are a little less perfect on the underside. RIGHT: A very good machine-done buttonhole that mimics handstitching.

Hair canvas interfacing—The best suit jackets have three layers: the fashion fabric, the lining, and a separate layer of hair canvas interfacing—ideally all the way down the front to the hem. Hair canvas gives a suit stability and structure. You don't need to take a seam ripper with you to the thrift store. Pinch the front of the suit near a lower buttonhole. If you can feel three separate layers, you likely have a full canvassed suit. Many suits use canvas for only half of the suit, and interfacing fused to the fashion fabric is used on the rest of the front—a cheaper alternative.

Suits made in France or Italy—Men's suit jackets always have a tag with the country of origin inside the collar. Suits from France or Italy, with their long traditions of quality work, should get a second look.

Inside handstitching—Well-tailored suit jackets will have handstitching around the armhole, where a set-in sleeve is attached.

"Pit pads"—Inside quality men's suit coats there may be underarm pads, usually covered in the lining fabric, to absorb sweat so it doesn't show through the jacket.

"Pit pad" under the arm. The handstitching on the lining around the armhole is another indication of quality.

Multiple pockets inside a suit jacket—
The insides of some jackets are filled with handstitching, multiple "eyeglass" pockets, and even a flap to cover the button on an inside pocket—so if you

Some ready-to-wear jackets, like this Banana Republic jacket, have flaps over buttons on interior pockets.

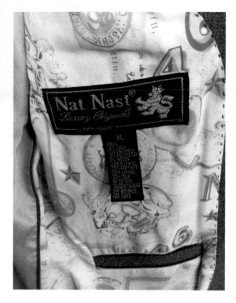

A Nat Nast jacket with a wealth of interior finishing: a welt pocket, finished seams, handstitching.

close the button, it won't catch on items you put in the pocket.

Handmade shoulder pads—It's impossible to tell without ripping open the lining, but custom suits often feature custom-fitted shoulder pads instead of off-the-shelf pads.

Fashion fabric under the collar—Most suits have the collar's felt lining exposed, but in custom suits the underside of the collar is often covered with the fashion fabric.

Thick, quality lining fabric—Silk is actually a second choice for a lining, as it tends to be hot and bunches up. Acetate is more often used. However, just because a piece of clothing is unlined or has minimal "skeleton" lining doesn't necessarily mean it is a poor quality garment. Seersucker, linen, and other warm-weather suits often don't have linings. Unlike in a lined suit coat, all the interior seams must then be finished, which adds to the cost.

Welt pockets—A thin pocket found inside and outside men's suit coats, on trousers (to hold wallets) and on

Interior welt pocket on a man's jacket.

women's jackets and pants. Men's welt pockets are almost always horizontal, but women's sometimes are slanted, for decorative effect. Welt pockets require more steps to construct than patch pockets.

Real cuffs on a suit jacket—Two-piece cuffs that actually button, instead of the usual three or four buttons at the cuff that do not button and are only for decoration.

Bound seams or Hong Kong seam finish— Seams encased with fabric or bias binding to cover the raw edges of fabric that frays. In cheaper garments the edges are bound by zigzagged threads done by a commercial machine known as a serger, or, even less effective, have raw edges cut with pinking shears.

Bound edges keep seams from raveling.

Flat felled seams—This is another method to encase raw edges of fabric while providing a custom finish. Used on jeans to make a seam more durable because there are three stitch lines. The process is time-consuming, so it is not generally found on ready to wear other than jeans or outerwear.

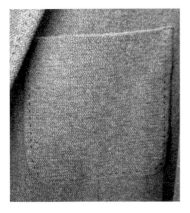

Decorative stitching, contrast thread— Each color requires time to thread a machine, so it's cheaper for manufacturers to stick to one color throughout a garment. Decorative handstitching is another quality marker.

Handstitching can be hard to identify, but it is usually slightly less than uniform.

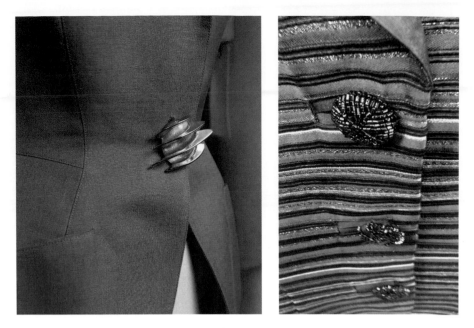

LEFT: Fantastic, futuristic button on a $3 Theirry Mugler blazer. RIGHT: Another example of a fancy button (and bound buttonholes).

Unusual buttons—We were drawn to an extraordinary jeweled button in a modernistic design at the waist of a pink blazer we saw at Goodwill, as it is something you would not see on a run-of-the-mill jacket. Turned out it was a Thierry Mugler blazer, priced at $3, which was likely less than the original cost of that one button. If an item has horn or leather buttons, look closely to see if they are real, as the originals are more expensive than their man-made reproductions.

Placket stitching—On shirts, look to see if the front placket (the vertical piece that holds the buttons) has top-stitching on it. Again, more stitching, more time to construct.

Specific sizes—Look for shirts with separate neck and sleeve sizes on the label (such as 16 ½, 35), rather than those simply labeled small, medium, and large.

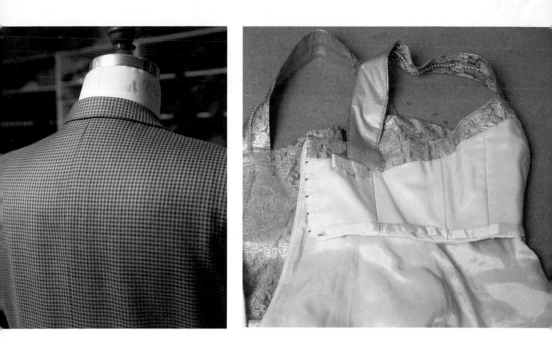

LEFT: The plaid matches perfectly across the back of this jacket, which is not always the case in cheaper garments. RIGHT: This Badgley Mischka silk brocade dress has a boned bodice that acts as a corselet. See it on model Jordan in the section in chapter 10 on special occasion dresses.

Full, separate linings—If a dress lining has its own hem and hangs free, it took more of an effort to make than a dress with fused linings.

Matched plaids—Better quality items will have plaids that match at the center front, on patch pockets, and at other visible spots. It takes more care in the cutting and sewing to match plaids, and skipping those steps is a common way to cut costs.

Boning—Whalebones are no longer used, but well-constructed bustier tops and evening dresses often have plastic or steel boning in their structured tops.

Weighted hems—A couture touch that is rarely seen in ready-to-wear.

7

clothing Rx

Thrifting is a team sport. You buy items alone, but you need a supporting lineup to help bring less-than-perfect clothing and accessories back to life. Through trial and error, we have found skilled professionals whom we trust, and we don't begrudge one dollar we've spent at dry cleaners, reweavers, dye houses, shoe repair shops, and tailors. Our team was assembled in Los Angeles, where most of the photography was done, but excellent craftspeople can be found in every area.

Their services are not inexpensive because their work demands time and skill. But in the long run, they save us money. These honest crafts-people will let us know up front if an item can't be cleaned, repaired, or remade—even if it costs them a sale. So we may be left with a thrifted $5 item that we thought could be repaired, but we had guessed wrong.

Sean Keklikyan, owner of Village Cobbler, in South Central Los Angles, a fifth-generation cobbler.

But we are saved the double whammy of a repair bill and an item that still doesn't make the grade.

Do the math to see if it makes sense to call in the troops. "You have to start adding up the problems before you make the decision to buy," says Des Moines Community Playhouse costume designer Angela Lampe. "If

Urania Blanco of Advance Dry Cleaners in South Central Los Angeles has been in the dry-cleaning business for twenty-eight years.

there is only one thing wrong—missing buttons, one hole, a stain that possibly can come out—it might be worth the risk."

Learning how to do simple cleaning and repairs—fix a sagging hem, sew on missing snaps, safely bleach a grayed shirt—can save money in repair bills and reduce textile waste. A recent study in *Family and Consumer Sciences Research Journal* found many millennials were discarding clothes simply because they lacked sewing skills and general laundry knowledge.

YouTube is stuffed with sewing and laundry tutorials, so you can learn these skills without retaking eighth grade home ec. A three-minute tutorial on replacing a button will have you snapping up the still-good clothing that the clueless original owners have ditched. (You'll learn

Virginia Astorga, left, and Ingrid Massella-Lopez, of Alex's Re-Weaving on Pico Boulevard in Los Angeles.

Kevin Samaniego works at Brothers Dye House in South Los Angeles, which caters mostly to the wholesale trade but will take items from individuals. *Photo/Allison Engel*

to use double thread, and make a thread shank by winding the thread around and around the underside of the button.)

One of our prized pieces is a navy Versace blazer that we found for $6.99 at Salvation Army. It had smart silver buttons, but three of the front buttons were

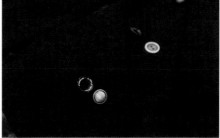

LEFT: Trim 2000 plus in the Los Angeles Fabric District had an abundance of choices for replacement buttons. TOP, RIGHT: The Versace jacket had three damaged buttons. TOP, LEFT: Costume designer Terry Salazar suggested nonmatching silver replacements.

damaged. After being unable to find a match for the buttons, we turned it over to costume designer and stylist Terry Salazar during our visit to a trim shop (see details of our visit in chapter 8, "From Plain to Pow!"), and she recommended buying a mix of silver buttons so we could keep the originals on the cuffs and two of the originals on the front. She suggested ones that were completely different designs, so it was obvious we had not tried to match them. Brilliant idea! Trim 2000 plus, a Los Angeles trim shop, had plenty of silver buttons to choose from. Four new buttons later the blazer is back to being quite the stunner.

New buttons put the jacket back in business.

If you graduate to intermediate sewing skills, you can confidently consider items that are drastically marked down owing to damage, such as skirts with a nonworking zipper. And you can start remaking or "upcycling" garments. Rachel Apatoff, one millennial who can sew, is a few years into her career in the costume design field in Hollywood. She has used thrift stores as places to find men's dress shirts that she remakes into perfectly fitting blouses. She does this by drawing what is known as a sloper pattern, which is a basic pattern made

The sloper pattern is pinned on a man's shirt and the excess fabric is cut away.

LEFT: A finished sleeveless blouse shows the princess seaming on the sides. RIGHT: One of Rachel Apatoff's finished blouses made from a man's formal tucked front shirt.

to fit a particular person. Hers is a bodice pattern, made from brown paper, sized to fit her measurements. She places the pattern on the front of a too-large men's shirt, saving the collar and front placket—the most difficult parts to sew—from the man's shirt. She uses her custom fit pattern pieces to cut the large front pieces down to size, then stitches the pieces together, making a curved "princess" seam over the bust on either side. She has made both sleeveless and long-sleeved blouses with this method, including one created from a formal tucked front shirt.

TAILORING SERVICES

Even for simple alterations, many shoppers prefer to find a tailor. Most dry-cleaning shops offer tailoring services, and there appears to be a resurgence in the number of tailoring shops—perhaps because fewer people have learned clothing construction in school. There's even an online tailoring service, zTailors, operating in thirty states. Free fittings are scheduled through its website. We found the shop we used, Orellanas Tailor Shop at the edge of downtown Los Angeles's Fashion District, by two time-tested methods: asking friends and reading Yelp reviews.

Maria Orellana, who goes by "Bertha," works alongside three other tailors in her busy shop, which is open seven days a week. She used to design costumes in her native Honduras, and she has thirty years

ABOVE: Tailor Juan Ixcolin presses a pant hem. BELOW: Maria "Bertha" Orellana does alterations on a dress in her shop.

WHAT THE PROS KNOW: HARRY MOFARRAS, DRY CLEANER

Harry Mofarras owns a dry-cleaning company that has been in business more than fifty years. He himself has nearly three decades in the industry, and at the urging of his brother, he went to a dry-cleaning school before starting. His brother has forty years in the business.

Mofarras says that for a competent dry cleaner, getting out grease, lipstick, makeup, ink, coffee, blood, food, juice, wine, and gum is easy. "We have a different chemical for each stain," he says. "But you have to spot and treat each one. Those discount cleaners that just throw everything in one load are not going to get those spots."

What is difficult to get out, he says, is glue and nail polish. Yellowed clothing is also tough to treat, he says.

His employees at Advance Dry Cleaners in South Central Los Angeles pre-spot stains, using steam, air, and vacuum to melt away as much of a stain as possible before chemical treatment. This takes time. "Quality is important, and looking carefully at each item, we can do three hundred pieces a day," he says. "If quantity alone was important, we could do seven hundred pieces a day—but we wouldn't get out the stains."

Sometimes, a complicated garment with lots of pleats will take ten minutes to press, he notes.

His advice for thrifters? "Find a dry cleaner that takes time with the clothes, who gets the stains out—and then give them lots of business!"

of alteration experience. Her daughter owns a dry-cleaning business not far away, and the Orellanas team does the alterations for that business as well. Her charges were extremely reasonable. Even our most expensive alteration—$90 for a man's suit that was altered in almost every way possible—was a bargain.

That suit was a pure wool double-breasted number in a muted brown and gray plaid, in pristine condition and well enough made to justify the additional expense. (We bought it for $3.) The wide lapels were dated, so in addition to taking in and shortening the pants,

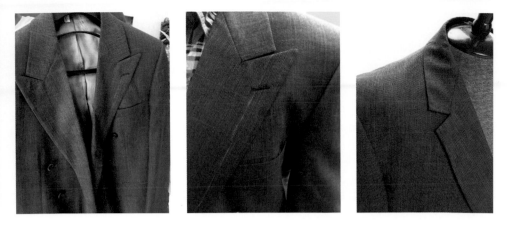

LEFT: The suit was made of lovely pure wool fabric—and had outdated wide lapels. CENTER: Tailors chalked where the new lapel line would be. RIGHT: The new, cut down lapel. *"Before" photos/Allison Engel*

shortening and tapering the sleeves, and taking in the back and sides, Orellana had employees Juan Ixcolin and Abelino Osorio cut down the lapels.

For a more simple alteration, such as tweaking a pair of thrifted Lucky Brand jeans so they fit exactly the way our model Alan liked, the charge was only $10.

Be aware that high-volume shops may not be as fussy as you are when a piece of lining needs to be added to a hem or a piece of fabric added to extend a waistband. Allison's daughter Nora thrifted a beautiful vintage orange coat for $30 in Palm Springs, but the sleeves were a little short for her. This find was

Pins show where the jeans will be tapered. *Photo/Allison Engel*

You can't tell where the sleeves have been let down on this vintage coat.

a fine candidate for alteration, because the fabric was a bouclé wool, with a thick, looped surface, and it wouldn't show a crease where the old hem had been. When we picked up the coat, we noticed that a piece of new lining had been added to extend the hem, but the lining color was red. It was close, but we wanted it to be a better match. Coat in tow, we walked a few blocks to the Michael Levine, Inc., fabric store, with its large selection of lining fabric, and spent $1.64 for a quarter of a yard of acetate that was nearly identical in color to the original. We then paid Orellanas to swap the small bit of lining at the end of each sleeve. Had we thought ahead, we would have bought the matching lining first. The two alterations brought the cost of the coat to $61.64, which included the cost of dry-cleaning. Still a bargain.

REWEAVING SERVICES

Tailor shops may be proliferating, but reweaving shops are a rare find. Reweaving is a time-consuming, detailed repair that is not taken lightly. Experts can repair most burns, tears, and moth holes to original condition, but you will pay for their time and skill. For a much-loved item that still has years of wear, it can be worth it. We went to Alex's Re-Weaving on West Pico Boulevard in Los Angeles, and benefitted from the

LEFT: Store exterior. *Photo/Allison Engel* BELOW, TOP LEFT: Samples of the reweaving and French weaving techniques done in the shop. BELOW, BOTTOM, LEFT: Repairs are so flawless that the reweavers put in stitches to show where the damage used to be. BELOW, RIGHT: Virginia Astorga, left, and Ingrid Massella-Lopez work on a suit jacket and a sweater, respectively.

many years of experience gathered in that shop. Two sisters, Linda and Evelia Escalante, started the business four decades ago, and Linda still works part-time with her three daughters.

We took in a 100 percent camel hair men's

This was the only visible moth hole in our $3 camel hair blazer. *Photo/Allison Engel*

ABOVE, LEFT: Red stitches show where two moth holes were repaired. ABOVE, RIGHT: Steaming the fabric had revealed an additional moth hole on the chest. LEFT: Our renewed camel hair jacket, ready for more years of wear.

blazer that we bought for $3 at Goodwill because we thought it had one tiny moth hole on the lapel.

Reweaver Janet Monzon used a steamer to check for other holes, and she turned up another smaller hole on the lapel and a third under the breast pocket. The charge for the repair was $90, and when she finished, she had to mark the repaired areas with a few red stitches, as we honestly would not have been able to tell where the jacket had been repaired.

The reweavers at Alex's Reweaving told us that steam heat, ten minutes in a dryer, or dry-cleaning will bring moth eggs and holes to the surface, although some moth eggs are so deeply buried that they may not show up until a second or third cleaning, we learned. (Cashmere, but not wool, also can be placed in a freezer for a day to kill moth eggs.) Patterned wools and tweeds are the easiest to repair, and gabardine and silk-wool blends are the toughest. About 90 percent of Alex's Reweaving's business is working on moth holes, particularly on cashmere. For rips, they use a different technique than reweaving, called French weaving. They find a piece of the garment they can salvage from a hem, or zipper facing, match it exactly to the pattern or plaid around the tear, and laboriously push the patch, thread by thread, into the torn area. For large rips, this can be an expensive proposition. We took in a pair of fine wool men's pants with two rips at the knees and learned the charge would be $220—too costly for the value of the pants.

We similarly said no to reweaving on a cool Dalmine Uomo sweater

TOP, LEFT: The two holes we noticed when we bought the sweater now had additional company—eight more moth bites. *Photo/Allison Engel* BOTTOM, LEFT: A well-stocked fabric store had exact shades of thread to match the sweater. *Photo/Allison Engel*. RIGHT: From ragged to rockin' with about an hour's work.

with suede accents we had bought for $3.99 (marked down from $7.99). We saw two moth holes on the front, but when we took it to Alex's, Monzon steamed it, held it up to the light, and delivered the bad news: there were six others on the front and two more on the back.

It would be $150 to repair. We had reached a critical point in the lifecycle of a piece of clothing. Now that repair costs were too high, was it suddenly trash? No, we got creative. Curious to see if we could tackle the job ourselves, we took the sweater to the well-stocked thread department of Michael Levine's and found thread that matched the shades of gray, tan, and brown exactly.

Working from the back, we darned the holes as best we could. The result certainly wasn't as flawless as the pros could do at Alex's, but since the sweater had a relatively busy design, you have to get very close to see the difference.

DYE JOBS

Professional fabric dyeing is another choice that requires some math to see if it makes sense. Allison's daughter Nora had a vintage blue 100 percent cotton dress that she loved unreasonably, even though it had been much repaired and still had a large impossible-to-get-out stain on the skirt. It truly wasn't worth repairing, and she had tried home dyeing with no success. (The stain still showed.)

Even knowing it didn't make economic sense, we took it to Brothers Dye House in South Los Angeles, one of the few dye houses in the city that deals with individuals. (Most are wholesale-only businesses, working with clothing manufacturers.) Kevin Samaniego, who works at the business started by his uncles, Alvaro Rodriguez and Rafa Rodriguez, a decade ago, was full of good information—and caveats about dyeing. "Everyone wants to dye it themselves, and they come in with their mistakes," he said.

Brothers Dye House and other professional operations use permanent

AT-HOME CLEANING AND REPAIRS

Here are some home cleaning and repair tips we've gotten from regular thrifters and clothing care professionals:

- When in doubt about stains, a good first reference is FabricLink.com, a site founded twenty years ago by textile expert Kathlyn Swantko. This trade-to-consumer site has 75,000 visitors monthly who seek out advice such as "10 Tips to Make Your Clothes Last." FabricLink has authoritative stain guides, laundry tips, and advice on fabric care products and storing garments.

- To spot treat stains, use hot kettle water, not seltzer, recommends Gwen Whiting and Lindsey Boyd, founders of The Laundress, a company that offers a line of detergent, fabric care, and home-cleaning products. To remove underarm odors, they advise turning the garment inside out and spraying it with a solution of three parts water and one part white vinegar.

- To clean cashmere, say the experts at Manrico Cashmere, which has stores in New York City, Aspen, and Vail, do not use detergent. They don't even use Woolite, although others do. To retain the fibers' softness, the Manrico Cashmere method is to wash cashmere with baby shampoo in cool water. Do not wring out the clothing. Lay it flat, gently pressing out the water. Let dry.

- For an oil stain on leather: Cover the stain with baby powder or baking soda and let it sit for three to four weeks. "The stain may not vanish, but it will be much less noticeable," says Joyce Sobczyk, who helps Florida clients downsize their clothing collections.

- Baby powder is also useful for cleaning the underarms and neckline of leather coats and jackets. Turn the garment inside out, shake the powder on, and rub gently. If there's a lining, it can be spot cleaned using a washcloth dipped in water with a little Dawn detergent. Hang the clothing on a shower rod to dry. Don't have leather garments dry-cleaned, as the fabric will harden. Most dry cleaners send leather items to a specialist, who may charge $50 or more per item.

- Unscented, alcohol-free baby wipes are a quick way to clean shoes and handbags, unless they are suede or a leather finish that shows water stains.

- Reuse those silica packets that come in boxes of shoes and other goods to keep clothes bug-free and dry. Put them in drawers and storage bins.
- To allay any fears about bedbugs in thrifted items, quarantine purchased items from the rest of your closet until you have dry-cleaned them or tumbled the garments in a hot dryer for at least ten minutes. Despite Internet chat to the contrary, freezing does not kill bedbugs, as home refrigerator freezers are not cold enough to do the trick.
- No sewing skills? To mend a tear, use fusible interfacing, sold in fabric stores. Turn the garment inside out. Cut a patch of fusible interfacing that's an inch larger than the tear and iron on the wrong side for a few seconds, using a pressing cloth.
- There are dozens of YouTube videos that demonstrate how to sew on buttons, stitch hems, and remove stains. Here's one that shows the running stitch, back stitch, whipstitch, and slipstitch—and how to sew on a button: lifehacker.com's "Five Basic Hand Stitches You Should Know for Repairing."
- If you know how to darn, sweaters with a small hole or two are no problem. The most important step is finding a thread color that matches perfectly. Take the sweater with you to a fabric store for the best thread match. Quilt shops also have excellent selections of thread colors.

dyes that are stronger and more permanent than the off-the-shelf brands, and they add fixing agents to seal in the color. Garments made with low-quality fabric aren't good candidates for dyeing because the fabrics often contain finishing agents that don't accept color well. Similarly, poorly constructed garments or those with much wear and tear may shrink or get damaged in the dyeing and drying process. And if a cotton garment has been sewn with polyester thread, the two

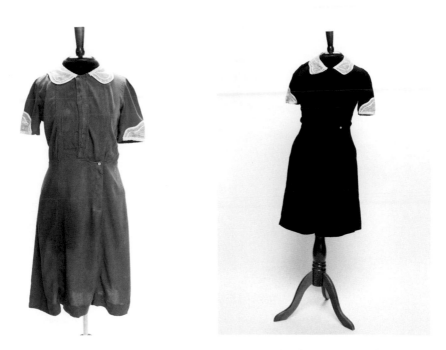

LEFT: A much-loved vintage dress had a large stain on the front. RIGHT: After professional dyeing, the stain was undetectable.

fibers will grab the dye unevenly, with the polyester retaining its original color. (We discovered this firsthand on the blue dress. Hem repairs had been made with polyester thread, and the tiny hem stitches came out a lighter shade of blue.)

Dye house customers pay in advance, so the enterprise can be a gamble for the customer, since the results can be different from what you expected.

That said, we gave Samaniego permission to dye the dress as dark a blue as would be necessary to mask the stain. We removed the lace collar and sleeve accents, paid $75, and in a few days, picked up a dress that was not perfect, due to its many original repairs, but now has a consistent color and is wearable. Nora was thrilled with the results.

Samaniego says that most of the company's business from individuals is for vintage items, or coats, or men's jackets. Frequently the

LEFT: The thrifted scarf was the right weight and length, but the stripes were not our favorites. RIGHT: After the colors were removed, the wool and silk scarf became a wardrobe item.

company is asked to dye a wedding dress another color so it can be worn again.

Dye houses also can remove color, and so we brought in an airy Italian wool and silk scarf that we had found at Goodwill for $4. It was a beautiful weight, and long enough to make a real statement on a coat, but we weren't wild about its yellow and white stripes. For $65, Brother's Dye House gave it an overall pearlized white color, turning it into an item that would get worn.

SHOE BUSINESS

One of the crucial members of our renovation team was our shoe repair specialist, Sean Keklikyan, who has run Village Cobbler, a repair shop in South Central Los Angeles, for fifteen years. A costume designer who

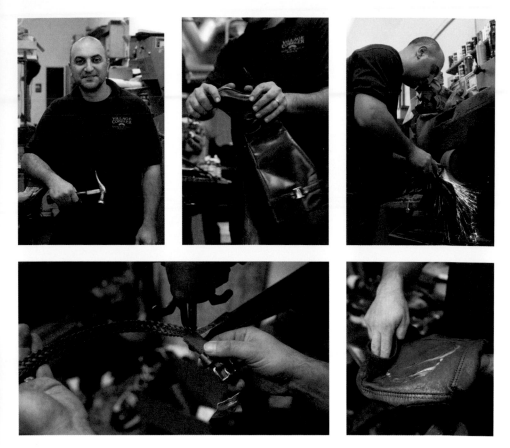

TOP, LEFT: Sean Keklikyan comes from a long line of cobblers. TOP, CENTER: Keklikyan puts a boot on a stand at Village Cobbler. TOP, RIGHT: Sparks fly as he works on a boot heel. BOTTOM, LEFT: Cobblers are adept at belt and purse repair. BOTTOM, RIGHT: Keklikyan can clean and polish—or dye—faded and scratched handbags.

relies on Keklikyan to re-create period footwear, calls the cobbler "a genius." Keklikyan repaired all the shoes and purses for this book, and he did incredible work making the items like new.

Keklikyan is straightforward about what can and cannot be repaired, and daily he has to break the news to customers that some man-made materials just aren't worth fixing.

"I never look at labels," says Keklikyan, who comes from a long line of Armenian shoemakers. He says that the only label he is interested in is the one that states that a shoe is genuine leather. Man-made soles, usually carbon or plastic, are harder to repair and can't be restored the way leather can.

"Labels can be fake," he says. "You can buy a Gucci shoe that's fake and it will be plastic. That's a zero dollar shoe for me."

Real Ferragamo or Bally shoes, for example, will have

We found quality Ferragamo shoes with one defect: a broken heel cap, on the shoe at right. *Photo/Allison Engel*

both leather soles and leather uppers. Those shoes can cost hundreds of dollars new, so if you find them in relatively good shape in a thrift store for $25 or less, they will be a bargain, even if you have to spend $15 or $20 to have them professionally polished.

We brought Keklikyan a pair of cream-colored Ferragamo low heels that we found for $9.99. They barely needed polishing, but one of them had a broken heel cap. Keklikyan replaced both heel caps for $8, and for under $20, we had a high-quality pair of shoes with many more years of wear left in them.

The cobbler urges shoe buyers to feel the leather and look for cracks. First grade leather is soft and supple. Third grade leather is sometimes given a man-made finish that will crack and be impossible to repair, he said.

The labels he does look at are on the heel and sole. If it is a brand that is sold to repair shops, he can tell in an instant if a heel, full sole, or half sole have been replaced. That doesn't mean you shouldn't buy the shoes. If the repair has been expertly done and the uppers are in good shape and can be brought back to like-new condition with a professional buffing, the shoes have plenty of wear left in them.

LEFT: These blue shoes with white stitching were in good shape except for the rough interior. RIGHT: New blue insoles brought the shoes back to life.

As for replacement soles, look for those stamped "super prime." They are the best quality, he said.

Another tip: Don't pass up shoes you love if the insole is nasty. Insoles can be replaced, often with better-quality leather versions, for about $20 per pair.

Belts and purses also can be repaired, dyed, and have scuffs removed at a good cobbler shop. We took in two thrifted leather purses ($3.99 each at Salvation

ABOVE: A Cole Haan saddlebag had seen better days. RIGHT: A polish and buff was all it needed.

LEFT: This classic Lucille de Paris bag was unusable with a broken strap.
RIGHT: Sean Keklikyan is skilled at making invisible repairs.

Army) that were marred with scuffs and faded spots, and Keklikyan gave us the option of having them re-dyed (a $35 to $45 charge, depending on the size of the bag) or having them polished and buffed (about a $25 charge). We opted for the cheaper alternative, and when we picked them up, we were stunned to see that they looked like they had been dyed and completely renewed. Keklikyan says that black purses are the easiest to dye, as others often require mixing colors to get a perfect match.

A classic black crocodile purse with a broken strap, also $3.99 from Salvation Army, was an easy fix. For $12 it was ready for years more of wear.

LEFT: This red Luti saddlebag purse had an ink mark and scratches. RIGHT: It looked like it had been dyed, but it was only a polish and buff.

Shoe repair shops often have the best selection of replacement laces, and we also discovered that they sometimes sell shoes that haven't been picked up. After shoes have been left for many months and the owners contacted with no response, Village Cobbler sells the shoes, which are, of course, repaired and polished. We bought several pair of Bally loafers for $10 and $15 each, and Etienne Aigner heels for $8.

No-shows are one reason cobblers usually ask for at least partial payment in advance. "People leave Gucci, people leave Prada and they say, you have my shoes as collateral," laughed the owner of Shoe Wiz repair shop in downtown Los Angeles. "What am I going to do with them? All I care about is getting paid for my work." He doesn't want to bother with selling unclaimed shoes, he said, so he donates them to a homeless shelter.

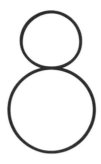

from plain to pow!

It started with a Dolce & Gabbana ad. The designers' fall 2015 campaign included a stunning double page spread of models wearing plain pink and black dresses that had large, dramatic appliqués down their fronts. Several of the appliqués were oversized red roses.

We could easily find plain wool dresses in thrift stores, we told each other, and then hit a trim shop to look for appliqués. So that's what we did. Los Angeles has an extraordinary downtown Fabric District that is stuffed with trim shops, but no matter where you live, there are many merchants online that offer all the ribbons, lace, appliqués, fringe, rhinestone trim, buttons, and cording you could want. M&J Trimming, a vital stop if you are in the New York City Garment District, has one of the best-organized websites. It includes a "Resource Center" with how-to instruction on utilizing trims. (mjtrim.com)

We quickly found three wool sheath dresses—one pink, one black, and one gray—at two Goodwill stores ($3 each on a sale weekend). They were excellent brands—Bloomingdale's, Nicole Miller, and Calvin Klein, respectively—and in top condition, which made them worth the time and effort to "upcycle." Upcycling is the process of creating something new and better from old items.

A pink wool shift from Bloomingdale's before "upcycling." *Photo/Allison Engel*

There are a number of relatively new companies devoted to upcycling, which seems to be coming into its own as start-ups start tackling the problem of textile waste. Examples include Sword & Plough, which gives military surplus fabric new life as purses and bags; and Reformation, a company using "deadstock" fabric, repurposed vintage clothing, and new sustainable textiles for its fashions.

Rather than do a slavish copy of the Dolce & Gabbana appliqués, we approached costume designer Terry Salazar (*Major Crimes, Angie Tribeca*) and asked her for her interpretation of the Dolce & Gabbana use of appliqué embellishments. Salazar, who apprenticed under her father, a tailor to Hollywood stars, is a member of the Costume Designers Guild 892 and the Motion Picture Costumers 705 (terrysalazardesigns.com).

OPPOSITE PAGE: **(1)** Appliqués are stored in narrow boxes. **(2)** Grosgrain and satin ribbon in a multitude of widths. **(3)** It's no problem to find the color and length of zipper you need. **(4)** Clasps and fasteners of all types. **(5)** Fancy appliqués for a collar, cuff, or dress bodice seen up close. **(6)** Buttons, bindings, lace, cording, zippers—inspiration surrounds you at a trim shop. **(7)** A selection of lace by the yard at Trim 2000 Plus in the Los Angeles Fabric District.

She has styled for Prince, big budget music videos, and rock 'n' roll tours, and ad campaigns for major international brands. We had more modest goals: a trip to a trim shop in the Los Angeles Fabric District, looking to make our inexpensive dresses look like custom creations. We met her at Trim 2000 Plus, one of the most complete shops, where helpful owner David Yag let Salazar try out trims on the garments. In well under an hour, she selected and "painted" with trims and transformed all three dresses. For the black dress, she chose gold metallic leaf appliqués, layering them with black satin roses appliqués and stunning rhinestone buttons that Yag brought out from his stash of special stock. (Even though these were the most expensive of his buttons we bought that day, they were still a bargain $3 each.)

For the pink sheath, Salazar found red rose appliqués and increased their profile by repeating them down the front of the dress and adding a few black rose appliqués.

The gray dress was improved with black lace appliqués overlaid with more rose appliqués, including one that curled up the narrow shoulder straps.

We spent a total of $49 on the appliqués and buttons for the three dresses, or about $16 per dress. We even overbought a bit, in case we wanted to make a matching necklace, bracelet, or shoe ornament with the same appliqués.

It did take a bit of time—but no special skill to tack down the appliqués after Salazar pinned and taped them down. We simply used a single thread and took small stitches through the appliqués.

OPPOSITE PAGE: **(1)** Costume designer and stylist Terry Salazar auditioning appliqués at Trim 2000 Plus in the downtown Los Angeles Fabric District. **(2)** Terry layered lace appliqués and flowers on the Calvin Klein dress. **(3)** The embellishments start to come together. **(4)** Terry Salazar starts work on the gray Calvin Klein dress. **(5)** Trim 2000 Plus graciously let us lay out the dresses in the shop. **(6)** On the black dress, Terry layered appliqués and added a few stunning buttons for accents. **(7)** Searching in boxes of appliqués.

LEFT: Appliqués snake up the straps of the upcycled $3 Calvin Klein dress. Katelynn wears it with a crocodile Lucille de Paris handbag, $3.99; a $5 non-vintage necklace; an Austrian crystal bracelet, $4 (all Salvation Army); and Steve Madden red patent leather heels, $13 (the Fairfax district Council Thrift Shop). CENTER: The Nicole Miller dress has reached another stratosphere. Irina wears it with a black tiger head purse, $3.99 (Salvation Army); and black Stuart Weitzman heels, $7.99 (Angel View Resale Store). RIGHT: Sophia in the spiffed-up $3 Bloomingdale's shift, with Valentino Garavini shoes, $10 (Central Thrift); Austrian crystal black necklace, $5 (Salvation Army).

All the dresses were lined, and we found it easier to stitch through the linings rather than continually push the linings out of the way of the needle.

So for less than $20 per dress, we ended up with true originals that could sell for many multiples of that price if found new in a boutique.

The point is, thrift stores are chock-full of boring, basic items that can be transformed from drab to fab with a little imagination and effort. At the trim shop, we had brought along a plain red angora cardigan to see if Salazar could give it some life. Did she ever. She started by replacing its nine timid buttons with oversized black ones. (We didn't have to enlarge the buttonholes, as there was quite a bit of give in the stitching, but we could have cut them a tad bigger, using machine or handstitching to secure the cut end. The buttonhole stitch, also known as the blanket stitch, is an easy and useful one to learn, and there are several how-to videos on YouTube, such as one by Professor Pincushion, which shows how to make a hand-worked buttonhole start to finish.)

Terry Salazar considers fringe for the sweater at Trim 2000 Plus.

Next, Salazar spied black tape with silver grommets in it, used for attaching snaps. Starting at the neck, she ran a length down each sleeve, giving the demure sweater a more edgy look. Snap tape cost: $2. Her finishing touch was silver kilt pins, which cost a quarter each, adhered to each shoulder. The entire redo cost less than $5.

We saw a fashion spread with a white shirt that had gold studs in a random pattern down one arm (retail cost: $710) and wondered what Salazar could do with the many varieties of studs sold at trim shops. We gave her a blue-green cashmere jewel-neck J. Crew sweater ($7.99 from Salvation Army) and a cute pair of cuffed metallic fabric shorts from Juicy Couture ($2, also from Salvation Army). She first changed out the ho-hum buttons on the shorts with silver and gold buttons that

TOP, LEFT: Terry Salazar looks at black fringe. TOP, RIGHT: Adding silver kilt pins at the shoulder. ABOVE: Auditioning replacement buttons and grommet tape. RIGHT: The angora sweater, reborn.

had more of a presence. She then collected a raft of square metal studs of various sizes in both gold and bronze, and arranged them around the collar and cuffs and down one sleeve of the sweater. "Think of the stars in the sky," she said. As a final touch, she added a few of the studs to the slanted pockets of the shorts.

LEFT: Terry Salazar looks for metal studs at Trim 2000 Plus for the J. Crew sweater. RIGHT: The Juicy Couture shorts also got a sprinkling of metal studs.

We bought a stud setter at a crafts store and soon realized it wasn't necessary. A flat-head screwdriver worked perfectly for tamping down the stud points on the fabric's underside.

We bought a lot of studs—about twice as many as we needed, it turned out. Our outlay was $14, and we have plenty of studs left to run down the arm of a plain white blouse that will look just like its $710 cousin.

Stacey wears the jazzed-up sweater and shorts with multicolor Nicole Club shoes, $7.99 (Goodwill); and a Bloomingdale's tweed wool jacket, $3 (Goodwill).

WHAT THE PROS KNOW: ANGELA LAMPE

Angela Lampe, theater costume designer extraordinaire at the Des Moines Playhouse, can look at a secondhand garment and see multiple

Angela Lampe.

possibilities. She'll spot an outdated woman's jacket in a bright nubby wool and not worry about the power shoulder pads or a missing button. She'll refashion the fabric into a trendy vest. Similarly, 1980s and 1990s beaded tops or mother-of-the-bride dresses, which can be found at every thrift store, are simply fodder for a knock 'em dead cocktail dress. She cuts the old tops apart and reworks the best bits into one stunning beaded dress, using the most elaborate beading for the center front.

Lampe regularly buys thrifted items that have useful trim that she cuts off to use on other garments she is making. Or she'll buy a secondhand item simply because it's made of interesting fabric that can be used for appliqués on another project. Collarless zip-front wool women's jackets, a staple of 1990s office wear, are particularly good candidates for repurposing, she notes. Sequined dresses from the 1980s can supply fabric accents for a current dress. "We do moments of glitz now, not the all-over bling look," she says.

Lampe has turned men's tweed blazers into newsboy caps, narrowed sweatpants into leggings, and turned out-of-date wool pants and skirts into fabric flowers that she uses as accents on hats or coats.

While at the trim shop, we were taken with a box full of appliqués in the shape of old pocket watch faces. They had a faintly steampunk look. We bought eight, at $1 each, and knew exactly what we were going to do with them. Early on, we had thrifted a white Pendleton wool blazer for $4.99. As we went to more and more thrift shops, we kept finding this same barely worn white Pendleton blazer. Either the company pumped out the same model year after year, or the blazers

For one production, she bought everyone thrifted white clothing and then used fabric paint to draw on details such as pockets and cuffs. You wouldn't want an entire wardrobe of this DIY look, but letting your inner artist emerge can be effective on an item or two.

Sweaters are particularly suited for refashioning, especially if you have access to a sewing machine called a serger that easily binds any cut edges. "You might not like that big, weird sweater in the store, but you can turn it into a stocking cap or fingerless mittens or even a sweater throw pillow," she says.

A quilter, Lampe hunts for 100 percent cotton men's dress shirts and cuts them up for quilt blocks.

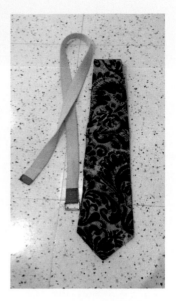

The elements that turned into a paisley belt.

The message: Be creative when you discover a thrift store garment with good bones but that is no longer in style. Think like a costume designer, who always knows there's a second act.

Following her lead, we covered a web belt with a thrifted silk tie in order to match the look of a paisley belt we saw on the runway. Our model Alan is wearing it in chapter 3, "Finding Your Style."

were ending up in thrift stores because they never became closet favorites. We tacked four of the clock appliqués down each sleeve and the jacket immediately took on an edgier vibe.

Looking over the rows and rows of fancy braids, beaded strips, and ribbons, we thought about collarless Chanel-look jackets, known for their piping or braid down the center fronts, at the hem and at the wrists. You aren't going to create a fake Chanel to pass off as real, of course, but that embellished jacket has been adapted so many times that it has moved into generic status. We've seen dozens of unadorned collarless jackets in thrift stores, waiting for someone to tart them up with trim.

Or how about making your own vintage beaded sweater, using reproduction appliqués and beads?

We geek out at the wide selection of buttons available at trim shops. They have a much larger selection, and the buttons are far cheaper than in big box fabric stores. It's no secret that changing buttons is the easiest way to upcycle a clothing item. For example, we found a mint-condition Jones New York Signature ice-blue

This blazer shows up repeatedly in thrift stores—without the clock appliqués.

Chanel type sweater in a department store window. *Photo/Allison Engel*

blazer for $3 at Goodwill that looked dressy enough for a special occasion—except for its light brown plastic buttons, which looked like they should be on a tweed jacket somewhere. At Trim 2000 Plus, we found cool silver half orbs with an etched geometric pattern on them, and bought three, at 35 cents each. For a little more than

LEFT: This Jones New York blazer looked dressy, except for the plain buttons. *Photo/Allison Engel* RIGHT: An easy fix: better buttons.

Tender Buttons in New York City, a shrine for button lovers. *Photo/Allison Engel*

$1, we changed the look of that jacket from confused to clear.

We are all in favor of "trim shop tourism" when you visit another city—the hunt can lead you to explore new neighborhoods. The items are small, easily slipped into a suitcase. A trip to New York City, for example, would not be the same if you didn't make the pilgrimage to Tender Buttons on East Sixty-Second Street, a citadel of antique and extraordinary buttons from around the world. As costume designer Angela Lampe puts it, "Not visiting Tender Buttons when in New York is like forgetting to see the Louvre while in Paris."

Trim retailers offer dozens and dozens of possibilities for embellishing clothing—appliqué crests, oversized buttons, mismatched buttons, braids and ribbons, beaded collars, feathers, leather cording, and so forth, that we recommend taking your plain-Jane items into a shop and doing a 360-degree twirl. It would be impossible not to get inspired.

Or simply leaf through a fashion magazine. Virtually anything you see in an ad or editorial feature can be duplicated by taking a trip to a thrift store and then picking up some embellishments.

On our same jaunt down Ninth Street in the Los Angeles Fabric District, we headed to another favorite shop, Journal Fabric, Inc. Our mission there was to find a new lining for a vintage blue knit Saks Fifth Avenue coat we had thrifted for $12 from Salvation Army. The lining wasn't torn, although it was a bit faded. We thought a new lining could give the coat some zip. We gravitated toward a print polyester chiffon, but knowledgeable salesman Ray Bolouri said it would be too sheer for the substantial weight of the coat fabric. He steered us to a soft polyester called Peachskin, which was 60 inches wide, and we found a perky geometric print that matched the coat. He quoted us a terrific price of $5 a yard (we had seen Peachskin online for $9), and we bought 2 ½ yards. With tax, our cost was $13.63, which is another reason why we love the Los Angeles Fabric District. With few exceptions, stores do not display price tags, and you are free to bargain for the best deal. Paying cash and buying multiple yards will bring the quoted price down.

We considered replacing the lining ourselves, by taking out the old lining, unpicking the seams, and cutting new pieces, but in the end we took the coat to a tailor. His charge was $65. So for a grand total of $90.63, we got a fantastic coat with a new lease on life.

Can't find a new lining to match? These days, it's much easier—

TOP, LEFT: A Saks Fifth Avenue coat with a plain, faded lining. TOP, RIGHT: Ray Bolouri, of Journal Fabric in the Los Angeles Fabric District, spotted a print he thought would work. BOTTOM, LEFT: Ray Bolouri cuts the Peachskin fabric. BOTTOM, RIGHT: Now the coat's inside begs to be shown.

FROM THIS TO THAT

Five years ago, Chelsea Confalone made her wedding dress using part of her mother's wedding dress, part of her mother-in-law's wedding dress, and off-white silk pieces from about twenty thrifted garments, which she used for tiers in the long skirt. On a seam inside, she stitched in small pieces of fabric close friends had given her as fabric tokens of love.

In the process, she was struck by the wonderful fabrics available in thrift shops. "New fabric is so expensive, and old clothes are so cheap," she observed.

The politics of the high volume clothing industry also bothered her. Instead of buying items that a child in a developing company may have made, she could make her own clothing and clothing for her children using thrifted items, she decided.

She began taking sewing classes and became a regular at bulk clothing stores around Los Angeles where items are rolled out in huge shallow bins and sold by the pound. She joined other regulars—the used book people, the people who run permanent yard sales, people who resell items on eBay and Etsy, and people who search for items they can consign or sell to vintage stores.

Chelsea Confalone makes pull-on pants for toddlers from the sleeves of blouses. *Photo/ Allison Engel*

and cheaper—to design your own fabric. A recent innovation has been the rise of services that digitally print on demand as little as a yard of custom designed fabrics. Now that custom fabrics are no longer limited to interior designers with huge budgets, you can turn your doodles and drawings, children's art, and original photographs into a wide variety

"If you walk in and look around, it looks like junk," she says. "But you can find really good things."

The stores put unsold and damaged items in the bins, among other merchandise. Clothing with rips or holes can be fine for reworking into other garments, as you can easily cut around the flaws. Confalone looks for women's blouses in attractive fabrics and makes elastic waist pull-on pants for toddlers out of the sleeves.

Or she'll look for interesting men's T-shirts and refashion them into leggings for her toddler son.

For her infant daughter, she makes rompers out of women's silk blouses, using a pattern she made based on a vintage romper she found. A silk blouse, even a Prada blouse she found recently, might cost as little as a quarter.

Hattie sleeps in a romper her mom made from a woman's blouse. *Photo/ Chelsea Confalone*

She also has found good fabric pickings at estate sales, including one fondly remembered sale at the home of a former costume designer, where huge bags of quality fabrics were priced at $10.

If you need inspiration or how-to instruction, Pinterest is a wealth of clothing redo knowledge. From this main site, under the "Explore" tab, look for "Remake Clothes." You can explore how to turn a too-small sweater into a cardigan, how to alter a man's shirt for a woman's shape, how to make a little girl's skirt from strips of sweaters, see endless T-shirt makeovers, and much more.

of fabrics. Spoonflower (spoonflower.com) has an easy-to-navigate site that offers nineteen base fabrics, including many types of cotton, crepe de chine, knits, and faux suede.

Our next project was embroidery. Digital embroidery machines have made it easy, and relatively inexpensive, to have a plethora of

TOP, LEFT: Embroidery down the front tucks of a Linda Allard Ellen Tracy blouse. TOP, CENTER: "Hope is the thing with feathers" quote on a Garfield & Marks jacket. TOP, RIGHT: "Mind over Matter" on the front of a silk Classiques Entier T-shirt. LEFT: We added to the one initial on this Anto Beverly Hills shirt, adding half of a quote on each cuff.

designs and fonts stitched on your clothing. At EmbroidMe, a nationwide chain, the catalog with sample designs is several inches thick and is organized with tabs.

No longer confined to cursive or block monograms on sweaters or shirts, embroidery can be as distinctive and unique as a tattoo. In fact, we Googled "innovative tattoo designs and quotations" online to get ideas for ways to liven up ordinary garments. Why not divide a good quote in two and put half on each cuff of a shirt, the way some people tattoo their wrists? We found an embroidery service in the Los Angeles Fabric District, SassonScrubs.com, a brick-and-mortar business that primarily personalizes medical scrubs. The owner was willing to do one-off embroidery on the silk T-shirt, white blouse, zip front blazer, and men's dress shirt we brought in. The prices varied from $18 to $30 per item, depending on the number of setups and words.

The storefront looked as low-tech as could be, but the process was absolutely twentieth-first century. Martha, the owner (she requested that we not give her last name), had us select our fonts by using our smartphone and going to dafont.com. Once we settled on fonts, thread colors, and positions, she e-mailed our order overseas. A template came back the same day (sometimes it's the following day), and her embroidery machine artist, Cole, finished the process. Slick.

If you want the creative satisfaction of embroidering a garment yourself, there's no better place to find nontraditional patterns than Sublime Stitching, a mail-order company founded by designer Jenny Hart in 2001. Her "alternative embroidery" patterns can be ordered for hand-stitching or machine embroidery, and include Martians and space characters, male and female pinups, Mexican loteria designs, and dozens of others that you won't find on your grandmother's handkerchiefs (sublimestitching.com).

Some of the processes mentioned in the last chapter, such as having a garment professionally dyed, can be used to spiff up a ho-hum piece. And shoe repair professionals can suggest ways to change the look of a shoe, as well as fix heels and soles. Our go-to shoe repair wizard, Sean Keklikyan at Village Cobbler, in South Los Angeles, gladly took on the challenge of adding metal chains to a pair of black short BCBG boots we had thrifted for $8.99. The square toe boots were in wonderful condition but lacked any discernible

Chains at trim shops are sold by the inch or by the yard.

LEFT: The thrifted boots and $5 worth of chains at the shoe repair shop.
RIGHT: Custom look, for a song.

style. We remembered the display of metal chains at Trim 2000 Plus and went back and bought $5 worth of dark metal chain in a size that was proportional to the boots.

Keklikyan fashioned a black leather tab on each side (so the chains wouldn't pull on the body of the boot), and attached just the right length of metal. Twenty dollars later, we had custom boots.

shopping aids

One of the most useful aids during thrift shopping is a smartphone. Carrying a smartphone can help you identify unknown labels and check prices for similar garments and accessories at high-end consignment websites. (See chapter 11, "Resources for Thrifters," for websites.)

Also you can use your smartphone to check designers' own websites for "how to spot fakes" tutorials. If you're on the hunt for designer goods, know that many, but not all, stores work diligently to weed out fakes. The forty-store consignment chain, 2nd Time Around, for example, recently hired a world-renowned Hermès authenticator who also has a deep knowledge of other luxury brands. The chain's owners note, "We believe in regularly educating our staff with up-to-date information on the ever-changing black market so they can quickly detect inauthentic elements, right down to the crooked top-stitch or the specific color of the tarnish on hardware."

Additionally, you can photograph the charts printed here on your phone that show the conversions between European, United Kingdom and American sizes in clothing and shoes. That way, you'll have them at the ready when you come across clothes and shoes with international size labels.

CLOTHING SIZE CONVERSION CHART

WOMEN'S							
US	6	8	10	12	14	16	18
EUROPE	38	40	42	44	46	48	50
UK	8	10	12	14	16	18	20

MEN'S (SHIRTS–NECK SIZE)						
US/UK	15	15.5	16	16.5	17	17.5
EUROPE	38	39	41	42	43	44

MEN'S (JACKET/SUIT SIZE)							
US/UK	32	34	36	38	40	42	44
EUROPE	42	44	46	48	50	52	54

SHOE SIZE CONVERSION CHART

WOMEN'S

US	6	6.5	7	7.5	8	8.5	9	9.5	10	10.5
EUROPE	36	37	37.5	38	39	39.5	40	40.5	41	42
UK	3.5	4	4.5	5	5.5	6	6.5	7	7.5	8

MEN'S

US	8	8.5	9	9.5	10	10.5	11	11.5	12	12.5	13	13.5	14
EUROPE	42	42.5	43	44	44.5	45	46	46.5	47	47.5	48	48.5	49
UK	7.5	8	8.5	9	9.5	10	10.5	11	11.5	12	12.5	13	13.5

GIRL'S

US	12	12.5	13	13.5	1	1.5	2	2.5	3	3.5	4
EUROPE	28.5	29	30	30.5	31	31.5	32.5	33	33.5	34	35
UK	10.5	11	11.5	12	12.5	13	13.5	1	1.5	2	2.5

BOY'S

US	12.5	13	13.5	1	1.5	2	2.5	3	3.5	4	4.5
EUROPE	30.5	31	31.5	33	33.5	34	34.7	35	35.5	36	37
UK	12	12.5	13	13.5	1	1.5	2	2.5	3	3.5	4

Another useful chart to have is a guide to designers' diffusion lines, so you don't get seduced by the name and think you have found a couture item when it really is a mass-market line. This chart is from Wikipedia, reprinted under the Creative Commons license.

DIFFUSION LINE	BRAND	NOTES
10 Crosby	Derek Lam	
Armani Exchange	Armani	
BDL	Ben de Lisi	For Debenhams
Cheap & Chic	Moschino	
CK	Calvin Klein	
D&G	Dolce & Gabbana	Closed 2011
DKNY	Donna Karan	
DRKSHDW	Rick Owens	
Emporio Armani	Armani	
Farhi	Nicole Farhi	
Giamba	Giambattista Valli	
Just Cavalli	Roberto Cavalli	
Karl	Karl Lagerfeld	
L'Agent	Agent Provocateur	
Marc	Marc Jacobs	
McQ	Alexander McQueen	

DIFFUSION LINE	BRAND	NOTES
MICHAEL Michael Kors	Michael Kors	
Mimi Holliday	Damaris	
Miss Wu	Jason Wu	
Miu Miu	Prada	
MW	Matthew Williamson	For Macy's
Notte	Marchesa	
Overture	Judith Leiber	
Pierre Balmain	Balmain	
RED Valentino	Valentino Garavani	
Richard Chai Love	Richard Chai	
See	Chloé	
Simply Vera	Vera Wang	For Kohl's and Harris Scarfe
Sonia	Sonia Rykiel	
T	Alexander Wang	
Versus	Versace	
Victoria	Victoria Beckham	
Wannabe	Patrick Cox	
Z Spoke	Zac Posen	For Saks
Zac Zac Posen	Zac Posen	

And, should you buy shoes or boots with plenty of life in them, but worn out laces, here's a chart to figure out how long a pair of replacement laces should be.

SHOELACE SIZES CHART

(These can vary with style, size and width of shoe or boot.)

NUMBER OF EYELET PAIRS	LENGTH OF LACES
4 or 5	36 inches
6 or 7	45 inches
7 or 8	54 inches
8 or 9	60 inches
9 or 10	72 inches

thrifting in action

PERENNIAL PIECES

They are the leopard prints you see year in, year out, the trench coats that are always a part of spring collections, the camel hair coat that never looks old, the summer stripes. Perennial pieces are clothes that are classic, enduring, timeless—and they come back season after season. Identifying these pieces is helpful to a novice thrifter. Not only are they the foundations of a well-rounded wardrobe, but they are guideposts to navigating a store, and, as mentioned in chapter 2, can give you focus while you are shopping.

Fall / Winter Coats

Thrifting coats is just smart. The vintage pickings can be phenomenal, particularly if you live in the Sunbelt or Florida where people from colder climates settle and give away their heavy coats. In fall, coats become the statement pieces of the season. Designers pull out lush, heavy fabrics such as velvets and ornate embroidered pieces. There is usually a rich, dark color that becomes the color of the season. For example, oxblood was a big color recently. Keep an eye out for the current season's "it" color by checking sites such as Pantone.com for its "Color Intelligence" seasonal reports, or blogs such as *StyleCaster.com*, which gives color

OPPOSITE: TOP, LEFT: On Nora: Camel hair coat, $9.99 (Salvation Army); Adrienne Vittadini sweater, $3 (Central Thrift); handmade wool skirt, $2 (Central Thrift); Ecco suede low heels, $5 (The SonShine Shop); Loewe lookalike purse, $3.99 (Salvation Army). On Bryn: Calvin Klein sweater, $2 (Central Thrift); black Levis, $3 (Goodwill); wool Burberry coat, $14.99 (Goodwill); Donald J. Pliner boots, $8.99 (Goodwill). TOP, RIGHT: Orange hand-knit sweater, $3 (Goodwill); wool DKNY coat, $8 (Salvation Army); black Levis, $3 (Goodwill); Sorel boots, $10 (Central Thrift). BOTTOM, LEFT: Vintage bouclé wool coat, $30 (Angel View Resale Store); leather short boots, $7.99 (Goodwill); patchwork leather bag, $13.99 (Goodwill). Underneath: Barneys cream blouse, $3 (Goodwill); handmade orange wool skirt, $2 (Central Thrift). BOTTOM, RIGHT: The total for his outfit was $24; hers was $56.98. ABOVE, LEFT: Authentic Navy issue wool peacoat, free at a garage sale that was ending; gray wool Alfani turtleneck from Italy, $4.69 (Salvation Army); Levi cords, $3 (Goodwill); gray suede shoes, $10 (Discovery Thrift). ABOVE, RIGHT: Outfit styled by costume designer Greg LaVoi: striped wool coat, $2 (Goodwill); lace-up Deena & Ozzy booties, $8 (Salvation Army); leopard tank and blue tights (model's own); brown bead necklace, $2 (Salvation Army).

previews in its "Stylecaster Daily" section. Color fashions repeat, so you frequently can find a coat from the last time that color was atop the hit parade.

Spring / Summer Coats

When we kick the heavy coats to the curb, there is still enough of a chill in the air and rain in the forecast that we require a trench coat. Classic trenches are shown every year, and although they are recast and tweaked by fashion designers, most trench coats stand the test of time.

LEFT: A nearly identical London Fog version in green, $8.99 (Salvation Army).
CENTER: Single-breasted London Fog trench without shoulder flaps, in hot pink, $8.99 (Salvation Army). RIGHT: A London Fog twin to the hot pink coat, but in burgundy, $8.99 (Salvation Army).

LEFT: This classic beige trench coat is by DKNY, $9.99 (Goodwill); Bally loafers, $8 (Village Cobbler); jeans (model's own). CENTER: A short trench, barely worn, $3 (Goodwill). RIGHT: Full-length red Talbots trench, $9.99 (Goodwill).

Color is a good way to get variety in trench coats. Once you make it your mission to find one, you will start seeing them in a multitude of hues. Shop during the $2 and $3 clothing sale days and you can have a different color trench for each day of the week for under $20.

Perennial Flowers

In the fashion world, flowers never die. The design scale may go from larger-than-life petals to tiny prints, and the colors from bold to muted, but a silk jacket, gauzy

Shirley in an unlabeled silk blazer, $6.99 (Goodwill); The Hanger red sweater and Linda Allard Ellen Tracy skirt, $2 each (Salvation Army); brand-new Karen Scott woven flats, $12.99 (Goodwill).

LEFT: Worn on Katelynn: a silk Ralph Lauren skirt, $4.99 (Salvation Army); silk and nylon Chico's shell, $5.99 (Council Thrift Shop); red patent leather Steve Madden shoes, $13 (Council Thrift Shop); filigree bracelet, $5.99 (Salvation Army). CENTER: Irina wears a pajama-top style silk blouse, $5 (Desert Best Friend's Closet); Massimo Dutti wool pants, $3 (Goodwill); Bruno Magli leather heels, $1.50 (Salvation Army). RIGHT: Sophia sports a Ted Baker blazer, $5.99 (Goodwill); handmade tiered taffeta skirt, $4 (Desert Best Friend's Closet); Tahari black patent leather pumps, $24 (Goodwill).

top, or skirt in a floral print you love can serve year in and out. Having a favorite floral piece in hand also can help tame a thrift shop's inventory. Bring that favorite item with you to a store and you'll have a laser focus looking for garments and accessories to make the item look fresh for another season.

Spot Check

Like swallows to Capistrano, leopard print makes a comeback each and every spring. As timeless as it is, the look will change season to season based on fit and the size of the spots on the print. So if you follow trends, you will want to see how leopard is being styled before you pull out your closet pieces. If you are of the "I make my own style" bent and wear your clothes with confidence and bravado (which is what style is really about), then wear your leopard however you wish.

Line Drive

Black and white stripes also show up somewhere every spring and summer. They are the definition of timeless and add a punch of chic to any outfit. Stripes are an excellent thrift store navigation tool because they literally jump out of the racks, so you do not have to spend time flipping each hanger in the rack to find them.

Timeless Topper

The white blazer is also another piece that plays over and over in warm months. Again, the cut may change, but if you happen to find one that falls into

ABOVE, RIGHT: A timeless dress that spans decades, Jones NY Signature, $8.99 (Salvation Army); belt, $3.99 (Goodwill); Donald J. Pliner black low heels, $8.99 (Angel View Resale Store). ABOVE: Stripes from top to toe. Alice and Olivia silk dress, $7.99 (Goodwill); black Armani jacket, $3 (Central Thrift); striped heels, $20 (Clothes Mentor); "pearls," $5.99 (Goodwill). RIGHT: An Anne Klein white blazer, $3 (Goodwill), works with everything from jeans to velvet pants; Mother jeans, $3 (Goodwill); blue leather bag, $7.99 (Goodwill); Vera Wang heels, $10 (Salvation Army).

A genuine army shirt, $3 (Central Thrift), becomes a dress with a belt, $2.50 (Desert Best Friend's Closet); over tights (model's own); worn with leather lace-up boots, $9 (Salvation Army); and a woven canteen purse, $4.99 (Salvation Army), worn bandolier style.

a sliver of timelessness and quality, you can wear it for years.

Military

Traditionally, military pieces hail from formal uniforms, but they now show up as casual looks with a bit of attitude and structure. Some years are bigger than others in the military look department, but it always has a place in spring.

Boho

Once summer rolls in, boho looks, with their fringes and nod to the 1960s, are perennials at outdoor music festivals. Think printed maxi skirts, lace trims, and shawls.

Other looks that come out in the spring and summer year after year are batik and ikat prints, pastels, and brights.

Metallics—gold and silver—are always on deck

This BCBG fringed top, $5.99 (Goodwill), became less sedate when we cut it off, turning it into a boho crop top. The Las Pepas Autentico Cuero leather jacket was a find at $3 (Goodwill). We paired this combo with a belt, $2.50 (Desert Best Friend's Closet); brown leather Newport News boots, $7.99 (Goodwill); and Hudson jeans, $3 (Goodwill).

and can be worn successfully in any season, depending on how they are used. As a general rule, they are worn selectively and judiciously in an office or casual setting, but there are always exceptions. For example, a metallic scarf or purse can work as well at 8 a.m. as it does for evening.

This list is by no means comprehensive. There are many more styles that roll in year after year. The point is that people who are into fashion seek out investment pieces that play perennial roles in their closets. They will then follow the trends and add some quick punch to their investment pieces to update their look. If you thrift your investment pieces, your outlay for that quality camel hair coat could be $10 rather than $1,500. Then, without breaking the bank, you can add variety, fun, and more quality to your wardrobe with thrifted accent pieces.

Seeking out replacements for favorite items can shrink a huge thrift store inventory down to size. Danielle wears a leather moto jacket by Ecru, $32 (Salvation Army); black suede Calvin Klein purse, $10 (Goodwill); Gianfranco Ferré dress, $8.99 (Salvation Army); and classic BCBG Max Azria leather boots, $8.99 (Goodwill).

One subset of perennial clothing to keep in mind while thrifting is "replenishment" items. As the *Wall Street Journal* noted in a 2015 article titled "Fashion's Secret Blockbusters," *replenishment* is a fashion industry term that means "an item is so well designed and constructed that it reliably sells out." Stores keep these items in stock year-round and year after year. The article mentioned a black crepe blazer and matching flared pants from Alexander McQueen, a leather moto jacket, a ribbed cashmere sweater, stretch leather skinny pants, a blouse from Equipment roomy enough to fit many body types, and leopard print pumps, among others.

Thrift shoppers may or may not find the specific brands mentioned in the article, but they can create their own personal replenishment list—the items in their closet they would dearly miss after they wore out—and keep an eagle eye out for their replacements.

WORK CLOTHES

Unless you are part of the lucky bunch that gets away with flannel and jeans in the workplace, business attire for the corporate world means "dressing for success" in suits, dresses, slacks, and blazers. Tailored business clothes can be very expensive, especially for those fresh out of school or the unemployed looking to return to the workforce.

Thrifting is a smart way to acquire attire that works for corporate America. As a matter of fact, this is such an important issue that some thrift stores and nonprofits have specific missions geared to outfitting people who cannot afford a business wardrobe. Desert Best Friend's Closet in Palm Desert, California, is one such

A wool and acrylic jacket with an exposed decorative zipper, from Hinge in Seattle, $4 (Desert Best Friend's Closet). Tyler wears it with a black rayon/nylon bandage dress, $7.99 (Salvation Army); leather patchwork Franco Sarto shoes, $1.50 (Salvation Army); and a red Monsac purse, $12 (Goodwill).

Men's dress shirts are among the most plentiful offerings at thrift stores, and are often freshly laundered. Even top-quality European brands are usually less than $10. The Domani Blue Label shirt with white collar and cuffs was $2 (Salvation Army).

organization. Bolstered by its motto, "Someone's future is hanging in your closet," the nonprofit provides low-income residents with "interview-appropriate attire at no cost to individuals seeking employment." Donated clothing is also sold in its store to the general public to raise money for the cause. Desert Best Friend's Closet is an excellent place to acquire business apparel at very low cost.

Similar operations exist in other cities, providing business clothes to residents of shelters, or women re-entering the workforce after years at home. Dress for Success is the largest, operating in more than 150 cities and 20 countries, from Albania to Singapore. Started in 1997 by law student Nancy Lublin in a Manhattan church basement with a $5,000 inheritance, the charity has helped more than 850,000 women toward

This Anne Klein dress was on sale for $13 (Clothes Mentor) and could easily be worn with a blazer. Here, Marzen wears it with Etienne Aigner pilgrim buckle shoes, $8 (Village Cobbler); and a genuine crocodile handbag, $3.99 (Salvation Army).

LEFT: The wool Claude Rap suit, made in France, packs a punch, $3 (Goodwill). Marzen wears it with a JS Collections shell, $3 (Goodwill); a quilted Diane Gilman bag, $5.99 (Goodwill); and purple patent leather Aldo shoes, $7.99 (Goodwill). **CENTER:** Richard walked right into this vintage Italian wool sport coat, from I. Magnin Design Studio, $3 (Goodwill). All-silk tie, Artisphere by Charles Vinson, $1 (Central Thrift); the RBM dress shirt, $3 (Goodwill), looked like it had been worn maybe once; the Jhane Barnes wool pants, made in Italy, $3 (Goodwill). Richard wears authentic, mint condition Mark Astbury Beatle boots from Liverpool, England, which we snagged for $19.99 (Goodwill). **RIGHT:** This French-made 100 percent wool pants suit has marvelous tailoring touches, such as inset color contrast at the shoulder. Labeled Dana Cote d'Azur, it was $19.99 (Goodwill). Sophia wears it with vintage-look G. H. Bass & Co. heels, $5 (Salvation Army).

self-sufficiency, using donated clothes. An affiliate program, Career Gear, helps men with business clothing and job counseling.

"All of the clothes are less than three years old and are something the donors would wear themselves," explains Lucy Reed, a supporter and sponsor of Dress for Success in Singapore. "The women's professional network here, mostly bankers and lawyers, has really stepped up with clothes and mentoring."

Recently, Goodwill of Los Angeles and actress/comedienne Amy Schumer teamed up to support women looking to style themselves for work. Schumer, who is an advocate for healthy attitudes toward body image, worked with her organization, Stylefund, to promote the idea of building up confidence and self-esteem by looking your best. As the Goodwill blog noted: "Thirty participants enjoyed a morning of celebration and transformation with fashion stylists and hair and make-up professionals. Each guest took home a complimentary professionally styled outfit and accessories and a new found confidence—to help them tackle the working world and create a brighter pathway to success for themselves and their families."

ThriftStyle went looking for office-worthy business attire and found plenty of nine-to-five candidates. Every thrift store has them.

STREET STYLE

Street style has become a staple in fashion. With the rise of social media, savvy fashionistas disrupted the glossy, perfectly staged photo shoots and runway shows of the mainstream fashion world and took their cameras to the streets. There they trained their camera phones on the fashions that people were styling for themselves. Street style is now a major influence in fashion, with numerous sites devoted to fashion scenes from around the globe. Some sites are more reality-based and show everyday people styled in their own clothes. Others follow fashion trendsetters: off-duty models, fashion editors, other tastemakers, and celebrities. Photographers catch them on the streets and also record what they wear to fancy events.

The Sartorialist (thesartorialist.com) and Street Peeper (streetpeeper.com) are premiere street style sites—the photographers/commentators

1

2

3

4

5

behind them have earned major success and respect in the fashion world. Now the websites of mainstream fashion magazines such as *Vogue, Elle,* and *Harper's Bazaar* have prominent sections dedicated to street style.

When we pay attention to street style, the realization hits that fashion tastes vary wildly around the world. Some countries' trendsetters prefer clean lines and wear clothes that are understated and chic. Others are over-the-top, playful, and daring with their clothes. Street style celebrates individuality and creativity. Studying all the sites we have mentioned is a good way to become acquainted with different styles and develop an eye for what turns you on stylistically.

Visiting these sites also can help you isolate different pieces that make up a look. If it's a suede fringe jacket that you are attracted to again and again in street style photos, use that item as a beacon to hone in on when you visit a thrift store. It's another way to cut a large, unwieldy inventory down to size. Here are some street style looks done the *ThriftStyle* way, which is to say fully thrifted from head to toe.

RESORT

Summer is coming. You have a vacation and nothing to wear. Get thee to the thrift store. To find the best selection, shop just before or just after the season. The pick of summer items is found at the end of summer when people decide not to pack things away for next year, and at the very top of the season when people are shopping for summer and clearing their closets of items that don't make the cut. If you shop for summer during summer, not only will the pickings be thin, but some stores will mark these items up because they are in demand.

Vacation shopping at thrift stores is a worthwhile activity for men looking to find casual wear that gets pulled out only during resort season. The guayabera shirt, a mainstay in Latin culture and a prized piece among the hipster set, is a perfect piece to thrift for. To make sure you have a quality shirt, stick to natural fibers such as cotton, linen, or silk. According to The Art of Manliness, other signs of quality to look for in a

Devon's cotton Alfani dress, $6.99 (Salvation Army) and wedge sandals, $11 (Goodwill), can't be pegged to a particular era. They'll do fine on any vacation, anywhere.

This embroidered Cubavera shirt, worn by Richard, was in mint condition and still had the tags from the dry cleaner's on it, $3 (Goodwill).

guayabera are at least twelve or more pleats on the front, fine stitching and embroidery, and sturdy buttons (see artofmanliness.com/2012/07/25/guayabera). A good guayabera is usually tailor-made, so be open to taking your guayabera to a tailor to make adjustments as necessary. There are also many guayabera-esque resort shirts that pick up some of the details without being 100 percent authentic. For example, our ramie and rayon version here has only six pleats, but it has two colors of green decorative embroidery and nice finishing details. It was $3 at Goodwill.

Another good find for men heading into summer vacation is a Hawaiian shirt. If you stumble upon a vintage one, you are in luck. They can date as far back as the 1930s and are a highly sought-after collectible. Collectors Weekly, a website featuring antiques and vintage items (collectorsweekly.com), has a detailed section on Hawaiian shirts in the Mens Clothing section. There you can find information on how to date a vintage shirt and confirm authenticity. For example, early shirts have collar loops at the neck, and shirts with coconut buttons are usually the genuine articles.

If you are looking for an iconic garment or accessory (Loden coats, Missoni knits, Minnetonka moccasins), the Internet is your friend. Go thrift shopping armed with some knowledge of what details to look for and you may score a real find on top of a deal.

SPECIAL OCCASION AND WEDDING

Proms, galas, and formal weddings are made to order for thrift shopping. You will wear that dress only once or possibly a few times, making paying full price a costly proposition if you calculate the per wear price. It's not that shoppers don't like their special occasion purchases, but they simply don't have multiple occasions in which to wear that winter formal or quinceañera dress. Impossible to work into a regular wardrobe cycle, they are one-offs, usually cast aside after one glorious night, living in the shadows in the back of a closet. They eventually get donated, so thrift stores almost always have a good supply of formal dresses and suits on hand.

It's unlikely that you'll find the perfect dress in your size during your first outing. This means you have to build in some time to work the stores. Develop a rotation of three or four thrift stores you can check often. An even better thing you can do is keep an open mind. If you want a black dress but you stumble on a beautiful blue one that is the right size and fit, go for it. As mentioned earlier, thrift shopping demands that you be both flexible and decisive. Now is not the time to walk out, leaving that blue dress behind, change your mind, rush back to get it, and find it gone. Been there, done that, and it burns.

Special Occasions

Special occasion dresses are particularly wonderful thrifted items because they have had limited use and are usually in tip-top shape. You will want to have the item dry-cleaned so, as with everything you thrift, make sure that the item is worth the cost in quality or sheer fabulousness to make the further investment in cleaning worthwhile. Tailoring is another cost to consider if the piece is not off-the-hanger ready for you.

To illustrate how plentiful the special occasion pickings can be, we spent two days thrifting at three different stores to come up with the special occasion lineup you see here. We purchased eighteen dresses. Fourteen made the cut for the photos. These dresses varied in price from $2 to $14, with most in the $2 to $3 range. While some of them may not be home runs, we wanted to illustrate what you can find relatively quickly. With patience and a bit more time, we are confident you can find a special occasion dress that will work for you. We're calling this spread "The United Colors of *ThriftStyle*" in a nod to the print feature done on actress Lupita Nyong'o in all the dresses she wore on the red carpet during the 2015 film award season. All the jewelry and shoes Jordan is wearing in these shots are thrifted as well.

Men also can get their special occasion needs met at the thrift store. So much about men's clothing is in its cut and fit, so a trip for alterations is usually your second stop when you're putting together tailored items. We wanted to dress our model, Greg, for a summer wedding and found a classic Brooks Brothers seersucker suit for $5 at a Palm Desert, California, resale shop. At a size 46, it was many sizes too big for Greg, who is slender, and he positively swam in it. Greg and the suit visited a tailor, who worked with Greg to give him the cut he wanted. The

Greg's too-large suit getting altered. *Photos/Allison Engel*

1   2   3   4   5   6   7

(1) JAX strapless dress, $2 (Salvation Army). **(2)** Coral pouf from David's Bridal, $3 (Goodwill). **(3)** Unlabeled fuchsia polyester dress with white accents, $2 (Salvation Army). **(4)** Watters & Watters 100 percent silk, $14 (Clothes Mentor). **(5)** Jessica McClintock halter neck dress, $3 (Goodwill). **(6)** Melissa Sweet 100 percent silk, $7.99 (Goodwill). **(7)** Turquoise Calvin Klein dress with spaghetti straps, $3 (Goodwill).

8 9 10 11 12 13 14

(8) Kicky Diane von Furstenberg 100 percent silk dress, $8.99 (Salvation Army). **(9)** An Alfred Sung polyester dress has the look of silk dupioni, $3 (Goodwill). **(10)** Beautifully made Badgley Mischka column dress, $7.99 (Goodwill). **(11)** Sue Wong lace dress, $7.99 (Goodwill). **(12)** Banana Republic one-piece dress, $2 (Salvation Army). **(13)** City Triangles one-shoulder sequined dress, $12 (Goodwill). **(14)** Foley + Corinna 97 percent silk dress with inset, $3 (Goodwill).

jacket and sleeves were taken in, and the pants were tapered. Greg is a fan of the designer Thom Browne, who designs menswear cut high at the ankles. This look is exactly what Greg wanted. (The original pants were so long that he had the option of any length he wanted, and cuffs or no cuffs.) So if you factor in the $40 tailoring fee, it means Greg got a quality Brooks Brother summer suit, custom fitted to his taste, for all of $45. We rounded out the look with a barely worn pair of penny loafers ($12 from an American Cancer Society Discovery Shop) and a button-down shirt ($2.99 from Goodwill). His pocket square is a vintage printed handkerchief (25 cents, found at the counter of a secondhand furniture store); and his rhinestone brooch was $4 from Salvation Army. We have to say Greg looks quite dapper.

Weddings

In 2015, the average cost of a wedding in America was $30,433, according to the useful site weddingstats.org. Geography mattered, with the average rising to $70,730 in pricey New York City and sinking to the relative bargain price of $13,214 in Utah.

The wedding dress alone costs an average nationwide of $1,259, not including alterations, and the price tag of many dresses hits five figures. Even for midrange labels, each bridesmaid dress costs an average of $175, according to costhelper.com. With figures like this, it is easy for wedding costs

Greg dressed for a wedding, his way. The suit, shirt, shoes, pocket square, and brooch were $24.24; tailoring added $40.

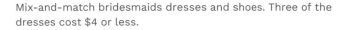

Mix-and-match bridesmaids dresses and shoes. Three of the dresses cost $4 or less.

to spiral out of control. Tellingly, weddingstats. org notes that nearly half of all couples exceed their wedding budget.

Splurging on an expensive wedding seems deeply ingrained in the thinking of many couples. Others would like to find a way to cut down on costs while still having a gorgeous, memorable experience. We at *ThriftStyle* are here to tell you, you can thrift your wedding and still have it be a beautiful affair. Why does that make sense? Because you will wear the dress only once (hopefully), and your

The bouquet cost more than our brand-new $50 dress.

LEFT: Tyler wears a Camille La Vie pink and black plaid dress, $4 (Desert Best Friend's Closet); gray and purple Beverly Feldman pumps, $14 (Clothes Mentor). CENTER: Stacey in a Miss Bisou pink satin dress, $4 (Desert Best Friend's Closet); Franco Sarto suede heels, $18 (Clothes Mentor). RIGHT: Marzen wears a One by Eight nylon and spandex dress, $3 (Goodwill); White House/Black Market open-toe suede heels, $20 (Clothes Mentor).

bridesmaids will thank you for not having to spend a mint on a dress that will molder in their closets. There's an interesting and hopeful trend to ditch the identical bridesmaid dresses in favor of different dresses that relate to each other. They may be in the same color family, or all be bright floral prints, or consist of various long skirts with the same simple sleeveless top. BuzzFeed collected images of mix-and-match bridesmaid dresses from around the globe, which illustrates the trend—and inspiration to try it yourself (see "31 Real-Life Bridal Parties

Who Nailed the Mix 'N' Match Look" by Melissa
Harrison).

This trend, of course, is custom-made for thrifting.
ThriftStyle took on the challenge, and put together
dresses and shoes for a bride, four bridesmaids, and
a flower girl for a grand total of $222.66. Even
better, the bridal dress was brand-new, still with
its price tag attached. We paid $50 for it—and the
original price was $1,038! We found it at the Fash-
ion Institute of Design and Merchandising (FIDM)
Scholarship Store in downtown Los Angeles—a
large boutique of student-made items and garments
donated by manufacturers. It was actually cheaper
than several of the nice thrifted wedding dresses we considered, which were in the $70 range, some including veils.
Good wedding dresses go quickly, we were told by thrift
shop employees, because frugal brides must compete with
others buying dresses for Bride of Frankenstein Halloween
costumes.

Our dress had the manufacturer's tag removed. It was
a simple long white satin sleeveless dress, reminiscent of Jackie
Kennedy's favored silhouette in the 1960s. With it, our model wore neu-
tral-colored strappy wedge sandals from Goodwill that cost $11. Two of
our bridesmaid dresses came from a resale shop that prices everything
in the store at $5. If you buy four items, the fifth is free. We bought five
items that day, so those bridesmaid dresses were $4 each.

The fourth dress, a violet lace number from Adrianna Papell, came
from a wonderful high-end consignment shop in Washington, D.C., Secondi. It cost $54, and might have been one of the cheaper items in the

store. Secondi specializes in designer names, and the store is organized like a high-end boutique. While there, we lusted after a gray Jason Wu wool sheath dress for $184, an Isabel Marant blazer in the softest, most luxurious burgundy wool for $322, and a Michael Kors yellow taxi coat for $679. These are not Salvation Army prices, but they are absolute bargains for pristine couture clothing. Our $54 dress was beautifully made, was in the color family we were looking for, and was the type of short cocktail dress that *would* get worn again.

Shoes for the bridesmaids came from Goodwill, Clothes Mentor, and Angel View Resale Store, a thrift store chain in the Coachella Valley. Prices ranged from $6.75 to $22.99. (Shoes are usually priced higher than clothing at thrift stores, but, paradoxically, the shoes often show more wear than the clothes. We have better luck with shoes in consignment shops or stores like Clothes Mentor or Plato's Closet that offer donors cash on the spot.)

The flower girl's dress was $5.99, from a Salvation Army in St. Louis, and looked as if it had never been worn. The Children brand dress was white, with a white satin ribbon under the bodice. To make it look like it belonged at our wedding, we bought a yard of burgundy satin ribbon in the same width for $4 and tacked it over the existing white ribbon.

Finding shoes for our flower girl required the most searching. The dress shoes we looked at in thrift stores were either black patent leather or the wrong size. Hoping for something in the burgundy color family, we tried ThredUp, the online secondhand merchant. Success!

Our bride, four bridesmaids, and flower girl are outfitted entirely in thrifted items, for a grand total of $222.66.

We immediately found burgundy DV Dolce Vita Mary Janes in our model's size, with sparkly low heels, to boot. (She loved the sparkles.) Price? $10.69, which included a 40 percent coupon offered frequently to first-time buyers. They arrived in days, nicely packaged.

Our $222.66 bridal party could have added a groom and grooms-men wearing their own dark suits, or thrifted suits bought during a $2 or $3 clothing weekend at Salvation Army or Goodwill. Suit alterations would add a bit to the cost, but it would be eminently possible to outfit an entire wedding party of eleven for less than $400.

11

resources
for thrifters

U.S. THRIFT STORES—ONLINE

- ebth.com—Everything But the House really is what you'll find on this combination estate sale/consignment shop site. Fashions for men, women, and children; accessories, jewelry, shoes, handbags, costumes, furs, shoes, and more are photographed and listed for bids, all starting at $1. The site buys the contents of homes and also features items that individuals consign. From cars to furniture, buyers from across the globe can bid and have their winning items shipped to them. Don't miss the "other" category in the fashion listing, which is where we found top label women's and men's shoes, as well as Hèrmes scarves,

L.L. Bean boots, and a vintage Bob Mackie mandarin silk blouse. 888-862-8750. ebth.com

- The website of the Association of Resale Professionals (NARTS). Its member stores, mostly single shops without the ad budgets of chains, are organized by zip code under the tab "Shopping Guides" and then by clicking on "Visit Websites." narts.org

- Showroom Finder—a listing of 366 consignment/vintage/resale shops in the United States, organized by zip code, but includes antique and furniture stores too. At the home page, click on the horizontal bars to the left of the "Showroom Finder" banner, and you will be able to search by state. showroomfinder.com

- Savvy Shopping Guide—A website that allows you to search by store name, zip code, or state. Created by Carolyn Schneider who has published an e-book guide to consignment and thrift stores. savvyshoppingguide.com

- The Thrift Shopper—A web listing that's heavy on Goodwill and Amvets offerings, but includes some solo operators of resale and vintage shops. You can sort its 12,115 mostly charity-driven thrift stores listed by city, state, and zip. thethriftshopper.com

U.S. VINTAGE STORES—ONLINE

- The Vintage Map—A terrific website that gives descriptions of vintage stores around the world. Its entries on Los Angeles, for example, run to five pages. thevintagemap.com

U.S. THRIFT STORES—PHONE APP

- ThriftBuddy—Let your smartphone show you what shops are within walking or driving distance. More than ten thousand stores are searchable on this free app, and you are given each store's address, phone, hours, and the distance from your current location.

SELECTED CHAIN THRIFT AND CONSIGNMENT STORES

- America's Thrift Stores—A chain of eighteen stores located in the southern states that puts out more than eight thousand new items daily. Offers daily specials, discounts for seniors, military, college students and 20 percent off your first $30 purchase when you sign up for its e-mail newsletter. americasthrift.com

- Amvets—Stores are located in twenty states, and their donated goods support programs for veterans and their families. A full list, with hours of operation, can be found at amvetsnsf.org.

- Buffalo Exchange—New and recycled clothing and accessories in sixteen states and Washington, D.C. Its motto is, "Outfit today, exchange tomorrow." Customers can buy, sell, or trade their items. Popular with students and millennials. You may sell in person or by mail with a prepaid shipping bag that holds 20-40 items. Sellers receive cash or can trade for in-store items. The Tucson-based for-profit company gives sellers 30 percent of the resale price, or 45 percent in trade. buffaloexchange.com

- Clothes Mentor—A chain of 138 franchise stores in twenty-nine states where sellers are given cash on the spot or store credit. Some stores provide personal shoppers. Stores are clean and well-lit, and clothes are organized by color and size. No appointment necessary to sell clothes. Clothes are priced at one-third of the original retail price. Sellers get one-third of that amount. The chain is owned by NTY Franchise Company, founded in 2006 by Ron Olson, who also franchises Children's Orchard (kids clothes reseller) and NTY Clothing Exchange (teens and young adults) stores. clothesmentor.com

- Fifi's Fine Resale Apparel—This twenty-one-store chain lives by the motto "Pretty clothes at bargain prices!" and has sixteen stores in Florida and five in North Carolina. Owner Fifi Queen has franchised her clean and well-organized shops, which focus on better brands in moderate price ranges. fifisconsignment.com

- Goodwill—The nation's largest chain of thrift stores, found across America with its smiling face in a blue box logo. Its motto is "Donate stuff. Create jobs," and hundreds of thousands of men and women find work through its centers. The national's online auction site is at shop-goodwill.com, and there are separate sites for "Hot 50" and "Fashion." (If you're near Palm Beach, Florida, check out the upscale Goodwill Embassy Boutique on 210 Sunset Avenue, 561-832-8199.) The physical stores have frequent sales, senior citizen discounts and 25 percent off your entire purchase after signing up for its Rewards Card loyalty program. Much of the clothing is organized by color, which is helpful. goodwill.org

- Housing Works—A chain of twelve stores in metro New York City that focuses on ending homelessness and HIV/AIDS. Women and men's clothing, décor, and artwork are sold in their stores and in reasonable online auctions ($75 men's Gucci overcoat; $50 Jimmy Choo heels, $40 Givenchy earrings). Winners have forty-eight hours to pick up items; nonbreakable items can be shipped. Its Long Island City, Queens, warehouse has $25 Buy the Bag sales, where shoppers are given bags to fill. A fee of $5 gives you a Power Hour ticket to get in early. shophousingworks.com

- National Council of Jewish Women (NCJW) Thrift Shops—There are a hundred NCJW chapters nationwide, with the biggest shops in Los Angeles and New York City. The eight Council Thrift Shops in Los Angeles receive more than eighty thousand donations yearly, often from estates. Begun in 1924 as part of the organization's Immigrant Aid Program, the shops also have household items and furniture. Supporters can upload photos of their donated items on the group's eBay store and choose what percentage of the sale price goes to the charity. New men's Cole Haan loafers for $25 and a $26 velvet Girbaud jacket from Italy were recent eBay shop items. The largest store in Los Angeles is at 11801 Santa Monica Boulevard, Los Angeles, CA 90025, 310-444-7978. Also 246 E. Eighty-Fourth

Street (at Second Avenue), New York, NY 10028, 212-439-8373. ncjwla.org

- Plato's Closet—A teen and young adults chain of franchise stores. Part of a five-brand resale group owned by Winmark Corp. This includes Style Encore, thirty stores that focus on casual and business attire for women; Once Upon a Child (clothes, toys, furnishings); Play It Again Sports (three hundred stores); and Music Go Round (used musical instruments). Cash is paid on the spot. There are walls of handbags in Plato's Closet, and personal shoppers are available. Clothes brought in for purchase must be clean, trendy, and in good condition; clothes must be less than two years old ("hot trends at hot prices"). Sellers receive 30-40 percent of the original retail price. The brand operates style blogs on YouTube, Pinterest, Twitter, and Instagram, and you can locate stores via zip code. No appointments required. platoscloset. com

- Salvation Army—This huge charity, in 127 countries, uses proceeds from clothing sales for alcohol and drug rehabilitation. Its thrift stores keep clothes on racks for one month before they are shipped overseas, shredded, or sold in cubes to textile processors. Its online shopping site, shopthesalvationarmy.org, takes bids and features such items as $65 mink stoles and $15 jackets from Chico's. Its trucks, featuring the familiar red shield, will pick up donations at your home. salvation-armyusa.org

- The Society of St. Vincent de Paul—Started in St. Louis in 1845, this Catholic charity operates thrift stores throughout the country. At the bottom left of its home page, under "Get Assistance," is a "Thrift Stores" link that lets you search stores by state. You can schedule donation pickups online. The Phoenix region declares the organization is "The Society of Second Hand Stuff Turned into Second Chances," because of the charity's assistance to the homeless and working poor. Shoppers at its stores are dubbed "thriftinistas." svdpusa.org

- 2nd Time Around—Approaching four decades in business, this chain of forty-one boutiques operates in Connecticut, D.C., Florida, Illinois, Maine, and Massachusetts (nine in the Boston area), New Hampshire, New York (eleven in Manhattan). The focus is on contemporary or premium designer goods, with clothes from the last two years and shoes/bags within the last five years. Customers can drop off items in stores, arrange for in-home appointments for fifty to seventy-five garments, or send in items, knowing that unaccepted items are given to charity. Consigners get 40 percent of the selling price for clothes; 50-70 percent for handbags, wallets, and shoes. There's also an extensive shop on Instagram. 2ndtimearound.com

- Stuff Etc—Large well-organized franchise stores in six Iowa cities selling clothes, jewelry, shoes, handbags, books, and housewares. Its mottos are painted on outside columns: "Secondhand is not a dirty word," "Why garage sale when you can resale?" "Fashion and frugal can be in the same sentence," "Wear it like you paid full price." Donated prom dresses for its Project Prom event are sold for $10. Founder Mary Sundblad began the concept three decades ago. The chain hosts in store charity fund-raisers monthly. Charities also register with Stuff Etc, and when supporters donate used items, the store credits the charity. shopstuffetc.com

- Thrift Town—This chain of clothing and housewares stores in California, New Mexico, and Texas proclaims that its fourteen outlets are "Your First-Class Secondhand Store." Since its founding in 1972, the for-profit enterprise has contributed $250 million to local schools and charities. Its inventory comes from donations to its charity partners, like The Arc and Big Brothers Big Sisters. There's a 30 percent senior discount on Mondays, an annual Green Prom Contest, and a Merry Thristmas Sale. thrifttown.com

- Unique Thrift Store—Red-vested employees organize and stock the thirty warehouse-sized stores with clothes, housewares, and toys. The chain links its free VIP card (offering 25 percent off on weekly VIP days and special e-mail offers) to shoppers at Value Village or

Valu Thrift Stores too. Unique Thrift Store pays charity partners for donated goods. Its stores are found in Colorado, Kentucky, Maryland, Minnesota, Missouri, and Virginia. imunique.com

- Value Village—A for-profit chain, headquartered in Seattle, that's part of the Savers brand, with 350 stores in the United States, Canada, and Australia. The stores buy goods from 120 nonprofits, informing their slogan, "Good deeds. Great deals." Its good website easily locates stores by zip code. Now in its sixth decade, the chain sponsors an Eco Fashion Week in Vancouver annually with a 68 Pound Challenge—giving designers 68 pounds of unsold items to create a collection, keyed to the amount of clothing the average person discards each year. Stores are well lit, with full mirrors in dressing rooms and attendants who will haul in your donations from your car. valuevillage.com

ONLINE THRIFT STORES

Primarily Mass Market Stores

- ThredUp.com—Children and women's clothing from better labels sold on an attractive, easy-to-use website. A bonus is free shipping, even for returns. Consigners are sent prepaid "clean-out kits" to fill with items and ship back. The site photographs, lists, and ships goods. Shoppers can sort products by size, brand, color, and price. Sellers receive 50 to 80 percent on sales of $60 or more; 10 to 40 percent for sales under $60. First-time shoppers receive a 40 percent discount on their full order. Goods wrapped in tissue ship in polka-dot boxes from California or Mechanicsburg, Pennsylvania, with a goal of two-day shipping. thredup.com
- Vinted—A site for buying, selling, and trading used garments, many under $15, from stores like H&M, Rue 21, and Hollister. Users upload photos and set a price. Customers bid, and sellers ship winning items, using preprinted Vinted labels. The free Vinted app enables users to

set up photo boards to focus on the brands and sizes they want. The site claims 8.5 million members and 22 million items listed, with its listers called "Vinties." The site's mission is "to make secondhand the first choice worldwide." vinted.com

Online Thrift for Charity

- WebThriftStore—This venture partners with charities like the American Red Cross, Generation Rescue, and People for the Ethical Treatment of Animals (PETA) to turn used clothes into cash donations. The inventory comes from donors who photograph their items, take a tax-deduction based on the selling price, and choose a charity to receive the proceeds their items generate. The charities pay the site 20 percent for hosting, plus organizing donors' shipping. "Let's turn all the excess stuff in the world into a force for good," the site exhorts charitably minded bargain shoppers. If the site's organizers are correct, the world is awash in $700 billion of stuff that we don't want and that ends up owning us. Prices are good, from $25 for a pink coral ring to a $150 Loro Piana cashmere scarf (retail $800). webthriftstore.com

THRIFT SHOPPING TOURS AND EVENTS

- Thrifting Atlanta—Founded by fashion blogger Keren Charles, who blogs at twostylishkays.com. Features monthly bus tours of thrift shops, a full listing of Atlanta-area resale shops on its website, discounts for shoppers carrying the bright yellow Thrifting Atlanta tote bag (a $9.99 purchase), and authentication workshops. It holds an annual Thrifting Atlanta Fashion Week, with fashion shows, visits to resale shops, and special discounts at stores. thriftingatlanta.com
- Thrifting Divas—Thrift fashionista Ayana Pitterson, of San Diego, organizes bus tours of local thrift shops and has twelve thousand

members of her Thrifting Divas Facebook group. This self-declared "thriftaholic" says her closet is 80 percent thrifted. "There is no shame in a thrifty fashion budget," she declares. She posts YouTube videos showing her hauls and discussing thrift store etiquette (no hiding clothes, no raiding another's shopping cart). thriftingdiva.com

- Thrifting Nashville—Thrifting expert Tay Singleton founded this group as an offshoot of Thrifting Atlanta. There are monthly Thrift and Brunch events, "swap instead of shop" meet-ups, sharing tips on its Facebook page, and discounts at thrift stores that host visits by Thrifting Nashville members. thriftingnashville.com
- Island Living Tours, islandlivingpb.com—Former stockbroker Leslie Diver organizes shopping trips in Palm Beach County in southwestern Florida, focusing on the multitude of consignment and vintage stores in Palm Beach and West Palm Beach.

PRIMARILY HIGH-END ESTABLISHMENTS (ONLINE, MOBILE, AND ACTUAL STORES)

Vintage

- Antique & Vintage Dress Gallery—You'll lose yourself scrolling through the celebrity-owned fashions (Streisand, Liza, Cher), designer hats, beaded scarves, 1940s suits, $15,000 wedding costumes, and so forth. Detailed size and condition descriptions and histories, with helpful label photographs. We've bookmarked its $150 section. Owner Deborah Burke has assembled a gallery of museum-quality pieces dating back to the 1800s, plus vintage lingerie, one-of-a-kind shoes in mint condition, jewelry and capes, sundresses, and cloches you long to own. Online only; 203-351-0639 (10 a.m. to 7 p.m. EST only). antiquedress.com
- Davenport & Co.—This Springfield, Massachusetts, online shop accepts layaways and has an extensive collection of vintage evening wear, hats, gloves, and wedding and bridesmaid dresses. The

descriptions are detailed, including measurements. 413-781-1505. davenportandco.com

Designer and Vintage

- C. Madeleine's—An online and well-known 10,000-square-foot consignment shop in North Miami Beach, sought out by designers looking for inspiration from the past and celebrities looking to impress on the red carpet. Garments are organized by decade, from 1930s onward. You may shop the website by decade, designer, or price. Most items are $500 and up, but the company's sale site included a Balenciaga fitted blazer for $198 and a 1980s Mondarian color block leather pencil skirt for $185. 13702 Biscayne Boulevard, Miami, FL 33181, 305-945-7770. cmadeleines.com

- Decadesinc.com. This is the online offshoot of the legendary Los Angeles designer boutique Decades, and it is a favorite for stylists with celebrity cash to buy one-of-a-kind knockouts. 8214 Melrose Avenue, Los Angeles, CA 90046, 323-655-1960. decadesinc.com

- Encore Resale—The original store, founded in 1954 by consignment pioneer Florence Barry, hasn't moved from its original Upper East Side locale in New York City. Located between the Met and Guggenheim museums, this shop, currently owned by Carol Selig and family, features top couture like Chanel, Prada, and Louboutin both in store and online. 1132 Madison Avenue, New York, NY 10028, 212-879-2850. encoreresale.com

- Ina—A six-store chain in New York City, named for founder Ina Bernstein, whose long tenure in the fashion industry attracts high-end consigned goods. Two stores carry only women's merchandise; one store is for men; and three have both men and women's clothes, shoes, and accessories. The items carry top labels, are pricey, and are either current seasons or collectible couture. Ina's online shop includes sale sections, with such finds as a Comme Des Garcons jacket for $375 and a Balmain blue metallic sequin skirt for $550. 800-462-1747 ext. 10. inanyc.com

- Linda's Stuff—An online luxury consignment site run by former attorney and admitted shopaholic Linda Lightman, whose inventory of 140,000 consigned items fills a 93,000-square-foot warehouse in Hatboro, Pennsylvania. The online site sells gift cards and has eight authenticators on staff to weed out fake stuff. The site charges consigners a $20 fee if items aren't real. Sellers earn 62 percent of items under $1,000, 75 percent for items over $1,000, and 80 percent of items selling for more than $5,000. She runs an eBay site as well. shoplindasstuff.com

- Luxury Garage Sale—Located in Chicago and Dallas, this venture also has pop-up shops and online sales. Founders Brielle Buchberg and Lindsay Segal feature mostly designer and never-worn items, with consigners keeping 70 percent of the resale price. Consignments are taken seven days a week, and store employees will come to your house and sort your clothes if you make arrangements at consign@luxurygaragesale.com. The stores are located at 1658 N. Wells Street, Chicago, IL 60614, 312-291-9126; and 6805 Snider Plaza, Dallas, TX 75205, 469-759-6200. luxurygaragesale.com

- Morphew—A vintage clothing archive and studio in New York City that sells high-end vintage by appointment and online. Aimed at collectors and designers, the store is a veritable museum of designer fashions and fabrics. Run by Jason Lyon and Bridgette Morphew, the site features items like a 1940s crepe dress with beaded shoulders for $448 and a $1,200 Emanuel Ungaro gown from the 1990s. 241 W. Thirty-Seventh Street #1101, New York, NY 10018, 212-564-4331. morphewconcept.com

- Poshmark.com—Social media meets online resale with sellers setting up virtual closets with photos, descriptions, and prices. This Menlo Park, California, company has organized national meet-ups for its millions of users and encourages members to interact online. Members can like or comment on the $1 million of merchandise uploaded each day. The site estimates it offers 400,000 closets for sale. Goods are shipped by sellers to buyers via U.S. Postal Service, and sellers receive 80 percent of the sales price. poshmark.com

- SnobSwap—Sisters Emily Dang and Elise Whang founded this virtual mall of luxury consignment shops so that shoppers can access inventory in nearly seventy cities. Shoppers can buy at the listed price or make an offer. The site has a team of authenticators. Consigners are directed to participating boutiques near your zip code. Items range from $140 Alexander McQueen flats to a $2,524 Chanel double flap purse. snobswap.com

- The Fine Art of Design—Shopkeeper Nicolas James Delgado creates inspired store window displays, and his inventory is just as compelling. Mint condition designer wear, including 1970s standouts such as Courrèges. Everything is in top condition. 73717 Highway 111, Palm Desert, CA 92260, 760-565-7388. thefineartofdesign.com

- TheRealReal.com—A San Francisco-based company reselling high-end women's and men's accessories, watches, and designer clothing. Consigners send items by FedEx, and the website photographs, sells, and ships them. Consigners receive up to 70 percent. Shoppers can pay $5 monthly for a First Look membership that gives them a twenty-four-hour advantage on sales. therealreal.com

- Tradesy - Founder Tracy DiNunzio has made it easy to turn your closets into cash. Sellers photograph and price the goods and ship them by prepaid USPS labels from Tradesy. The website's I-phone app lets sellers list in seconds. Designer replicas are kept off the site with knock-off detection technology, and buyers are given money-back authenticity guarantees. There are no re-stocking fees for returns. There is a large trade in wedding gowns, plus brands like Tory Burch, Rag & Bone, Tiffany, and BCBG. Sellers receive 88 percent in cash or 91 percent in store credit. tradesy.com

- Vaunte—Shop the closets of stylists in this online reseller that features in-the-moment fashions at very reduced prices. Sellers submit pieces for review to its New York City headquarters, where accepted pieces are photographed for the site. The commission taken is 40 percent. Closets are featured, like that of Dallas-based stylist Nini Nguyen, with 83,000 Instagram followers. You can buy her size 6 Thierry Mugler dress for $179 (originally $1,995), and Yves Saint Laurent pants for $80. vaunte.com

- Vestiaire Collective. A Paris-based luxury resale company with a dozen authenticators on staff to ensure the Birkin bags and Chanel skirts are genuine. The "pre-loved" handbags and designer fashions are 30 to 70 percent off original prices, but very little on the site is under $500. There's a "wear now, pay later" installment plan option. vestiairecollective.com

- Vintage Martini—Co-owners Ken Weber and Greg Kelly began selling vintage via website in 1999 and established an actual store in 2007. Clothes are consigned for four months, commissions are split fifty-fifty, and consigners receive a "farewell" letter about unsold merchandise. The top-quality offerings range from Victorian and Edwardian to current designer fashions. The owners will travel out of state to evaluate consignments of more than 100 items. Weber, who has a degree in costume design, blogs about vintage for DFW Style Daily, the Dallas area's fashion and style news site. Vintage Martini clothes also have been part of Fashion X Dallas, the city's annual fashion show. 2923 N. Henderson Avenue, Dallas, TX 75206, 469-334-0584. vintagemartini.com

ITEM-SPECIFIC VINTAGE STORES

Wedding

- Mill Crest Vintage—This Lambertville, New Jersey, shop organizes its beautifully kept gowns by decade, back to the 1920s. Dresses range from $200 to $1,100, with most in the $400-$600 range. All sales are final. Most of the company's business is online, and it ships to Canada, EU, Australia, New Zealand, Switzerland, Norway, and Japan. Brides in the NYC/Philly region can make appointments and easily visit the store. 72 Bridge Street, Lambertville, NJ 08530, 609-397-4700. millcrestvintage.com

Hawaiian Shirts

- Vintage Aloha Shirts—A staggering number of authentic shirts of old Hawaii (especially 1930-1950), which you can sort by size, price, manufacturer, and material. Prices range from $19 to $1,900. The old rayon shirts, called "silkies," are most prized as wearable works of art. The company stores shirts in acid free paper inside vacuum-sealed bags with silica gel packs to counteract Hawaii's humidity, which can lead to foxing and mold. vintage-aloha-shirt.com

Shoes and Boots

- The Cats Pajamas—In its fourth decade of vintage offerings, this online store has several uncommon categories, including footwear and curvy girl clothing and kids' vintage. (There is a similarly named website, The Cat's Pajamas, which sells pajamas.) A section of items priced at $25 and under offers mostly ties, belts, and fabrics. You may visit its actual store by appointment only. 2900 Orchard Avenue, Montoursville, PA 17754, 570-322-5580. catspajamas.com

Jewelry

- Carol Lane Antiques—This Riverdale, New York, online dealer specializes in very high-end estate jewelry, from Victorian to Arts and Crafts, Scandinavian, and Art Nouveau. 914-523-9222. laneantiques.com
- Isadoras Antique Jewelry—Based in Seattle, this site and store offers vintage rings, cuff links, brooches, bracelets, necklaces, and so forth. Prices range from a garnet crown brooch for $475 to diamond

Art Deco engagement rings for $8,100. Shipping is free within the United States. 1601 First Avenue, Seattle, WA 98101, 206-441-7711. isadoras.com

- Millsboro Bazaar—A cornucopia of costume jewelry, organized by color, design, and era. Although the amount of neatly labeled jewelry is staggering, this business, located at a former funeral home, also sells vintage clothing and accessories. No online or mail order sales. 238 Main Street, Millsboro, DE 19966, 302-934-7413. Closed Thursdays.

VINTAGE CLOTHING SHOWS

- Manhattan Vintage Clothing Show and Sale—Held three times yearly, plus a Gentlemen's Vintage Show. Held at the Metropolitan Pavilion, 125 W. Eighteenth Street, New York, NY 10011, 518-434-4312. manhattanvintage.com
- Vintage Fashion Expo—A collection of fifty vintage vendors that takes place five times yearly in Los Angeles (three shows) and San Francisco (two shows). Clothing ranges from the eighteenth-century to the 1990s. These two-day shows have been held for thirty years. The Reef, 1933 S. Broadway, Los Angeles, CA 90007; County Fair Building, 1199 Ninth Avenue, San Francisco, CA 94122. vintageexpo.com
- Vintage Garage Chicago—More than a hundred Midwest dealers fill a large parking garage seven times yearly (from April through October), on the third Sunday of the month. Clothing and accessories are joined by decor and furniture. The organizer also runs vintage shows in Dallas and Grand Rapids, Michigan. Vintage Promotions, LLC, 5051 N. Broadway, Chicago, IL 60640, 817-579-9079. vintage-promotionsllc.com

AUCTIONS

- Heritage Auctions—Best known for sports memorabilia, fine watches, rare coins, and celebrity estates, this large Dallas-based enterprise also includes luxury handbags in its auctions. Amid the $21,000 Birkin bags there have been winning bids of $55 for a Bottega Veneta bag and a $150 Dior shoulder purse. ha.com

CLOTHING TRADESPEOPLE

- Modern Leather Goods—A New York City mainstay since 1944, this shop will reline purses, repair handbag zippers, and renovate shoes. 2 W. Thirty-Second Street, 4th Floor, New York, NY 10001, 212-279-3263. modernleathergoods.com
- Without a Trace—Renovates leather purses, furs, Ugg boots, plus reweaving wool and reknitting flaws in sweaters. They create custom headbands from outdated fur items. If you're not near its two locations in Chicago, you may ship in your goods needing repair. 3344 W. Bryn Mawr Avenue, Chicago, IL 60659, 773 588-4922; and 100 E. Walton Street, Chicago, IL 60611, 312-787-9922. withoutatrace.com
- zTailors—An online tailoring service now in twenty-nine states plus the District of Columbia, and fifty cities. You can schedule free fittings through the website at your home or office. Tailors handle one item or a wardrobe, and most items are returned within a week. ztailors.com

CLOTHING ASSOCIATIONS

- Costume Society of America—Focuses on education, research, preservation, and design of clothes, and publishes a journal, *Dress: The Journal of the Costume Society of America*, which features articles, book and exhibition reviews, letters to the editor, and short reports. costumesocietyamerica.com

- Vintage Fashion Guild—Since 2002, this association of vintage clothing dealers, fashion historians, and stylists has offered free "Resource Libraries" to identify vintage labels, fabrics, fur and exotic skins, hats, lingerie, and so forth, with photographs and detailed descriptions, as well as a "Fashion Timeline." Its website links to members' shops, blogs, and web shops. Click on "Shop VFG member stores" and you will find lists with links to a multitude of actual stores and online stores. vintagefashionguild.org

BLOGS AND FASHION SITES

- Chronically Vintage—This site interviews designers, has a YouTube channel, an online shop, vintage recipes, and links to helpful sites like We Heart Vintage Directory, The Vintage Map, Blue Velvet Vintage and the unusual Etsy shop of Baltimorean Janine D'Agati and her Guermanes Antique and Vintage Clothing offerings can be found by clicking the "Links" button at the top of the main web page. chronicallyvintage.com
- A Thick Girl's Closet—Shay Tucker celebrates plus-size fashionistas on her blog, which appears on many platforms, including Facebook, tumblr, Pinterest, and YouTube. athickgirlscloset.com
- Looking Fly on a Dime—Blogger and author Patrice J. Williams challenges herself and others not to buy new clothes/accessories for a year in her blog ThriftyThreads365. In 2012 she spent less than $500; in 2014, just $233! She advises thrifting newbies in her e-book and shares her finds and looks on most social media platforms. lookingflyonadime.com
- Refashionista—Blogger Jillian Owens uses attractive before, during, and after photos, with close-ups of sewing techniques, to show you how to remake frumpy or thrifted clothes into cool and unique new

fashions. Her equation is ReFashion=Fashion Revisited, Repurposed, and Revitalized. By detailing how to create miniskirts from sweaters and eye-catching tops from bland dresses, her blog is a DIY and eco-fashion find. refashionista.net

- StyleCaster—a fashion and celebrity site that gives fashion previews in its "Stylecaster Daily" section under the "Fashion" tab. Useful for checking out what colors are going to be in fashion for an upcoming season. stylecaster.com
- Tales from the Thrift—New Yorker Christina Jelski estimates that 75 percent of her closet is from thrift and consignment shops. Her blog is a guide to her hauls and favorite shops in a city filled with resellers and fashion fiends. talesfromthethrift.com
- The Budget Babe—Useful for its "Celebrity Style" feature where celebrities' fashion looks are shown with bargain alternatives that achieve a similar look. Editor Dianna Baros and her contributors aim for "fab without a fortune." thebudgetbabe.com
- The Cheap Chick—Based in the Minneapolis area, but with advice for all thrifters, this blogger is a frugal living expert. She sets challenges, such as spending less than $20 on all items for a year, or requiring shoppers to have "3 Reasons Why to Buy" any item. thecheapchick. com
- Vintage Vandalizm—Jasmin Rodriguez, a New Yorker now in Las Vegas working for neo-retro Pinup Girl Clothing, writes about vintage, but also about 1950s culture, old Hollywood, rockabilly style, and more. vintagevandalizm.com

FABRICS

- B. Black & Sons—In business in Los Angeles since 1922, B. Black has "the world's finest woolens and tailoring supplies" at its store in the Fabric District, and its offerings are available online. Beyond an exhaustive selection of wools, it has silk matka, shirting cottons, and linen. 548 S. Los Angeles Street, Los Angeles, CA 90013, 213-624-9451 bblackandsons.com

- Britex Fabrics—Trying to match a fabric or trim? Britex has a well-organized service that sends 2x4-inch swatches of the fabrics it displays online for $1 per swatch (plus shipping), and offers swatches of ribbon, lace and other trims as well. Its blog, which can be accessed by clicking "Blog" at the top of the company's web page, includes tutorials (how to make harem pants, neckties, hem with rayon seam binding, and many more) and projects made by customers and staffers. The company's historic four-story store near Union Square is a must-stop when in San Francisco. 146 Geary Street, San Francisco, CA 94108, 415-392-2910. britexfabrics.com

- Mood Fabrics—Its mother ship in Manhattan covers three floors in the Garment District. Its newer outlet is in the Mid-Wilshire neighborhood of Los Angeles. Or shop on its excellent website, which includes a "Shop the Look" feature, where you can browse designs from Project Runway and buy the very fabrics used to create them. 225 W. Thirty-Seventh Street, 3rd Floor, New York, NY 10018, 212-730-5003; and 645 S. La Brea Avenue, Los Angeles, CA 90036, 323-653-6663. moodfabrics.com

- Quilt shops—There are thousands of locally owned quilt shops across the nation, and several sites include locaters or state-by-state lists. Many shops offer online ordering of quilt patterns, notions, wools, and 100 percent cotton fabrics that you will never see in the big chain fabric stores. Find a store near you at allpeoplequilt.com by clicking on the "Shopping" tab and selecting "Quilt Shop Locator"; or at generations-quilt-patterns.com under "Directories—Find or List" select "Quilt Stores." You will be able to search for places where you can find lovely 100 percent cotton fabrics, wools, and specialty threads. There are thousands of locally owned shops across the nation, carrying inventory you'll never see in the big chain fabric stores. Most shops sell by mail via their websites. Find a store near you by going to allpeoplequilt.com, selecting the "Shopping" tab at the top, and clicking on "Quilt Shop Locator."

- Keepsake Quilting—This New Hampshire store has one of the largest online stores. On the Keepsake site, you can search by color (sixty-four different green fabrics, eighty-three different blues, and so forth), as well as by theme, manufacturer, and fabric type. Quilt fabric designs include a healthy selection of reproduction fabrics of various eras—Civil War through the 1980s—which can come in handy when you are looking for something to match a vintage find. 12 Main Street, Center Harbor, NH 03226, 603-253-4026. keepsakequilting.com

- Spoonflower—This custom fabric design service encourages individuals to upload their designs so that others can purchase them. This service provides the largest collection of independent fabric designers in the world. It offers nineteen base fabrics (including many types of cotton, crepe de Chine, performance knit, jersey, Lycra, and faux suede), as well as wallpaper and gift wrap that can be custom printed. Watch a video about the service at the "About Us" page on the website. You can search designs by dozens of subjects (steampunk, butterfly, Medieval, Halloween, etc.) or browse page after page of clever designs. Sew-ins and instructional events are held at its headquarters. 2810 Meridian Parkway, Suite 176, Durham, NC 27713, 919-886-7885. spoonflower.com

FABRIC CARE

- FabricLink—Includes stain guides, laundry tips, fabric care products, and advice on storing garments. Founded twenty years ago by textile expert Kathlyn Swantko, this trade-to-consumer site has 75,000 visitors monthly who seek out advice like "Ten Tips to Make Your Clothes Last," which includes useful information on garment construction. fabriclink.com

SEWING AND DIY HELP

- Sew-Hip—Lots of sewing blogs aren't kept up, but this one is a good place for people to request help from a sewing community that stays current. Its motto is "This ain't your grandma's sewing circle." sew-hip .livejournal.com

TRIMS

- Benno's Buttons—A Dallas, Texas, storefront shop with an extensive collection of buttons and trimmings, including bridal ribbon; suit and coat buttons; frogs and toggles; buttons made of leather, metal, rhinestone; and novelty buttons. A good search function enables you to shop online for exactly the button you're missing. 12300 Inwood Road, #106, Dallas, TX 75244, 214-634-2324. bennosbuttons.com
- M & J Trimming—This store in New York City's Garment District is a wonderland of trims, and its excellent website has a good selection of its inventory online. The company ships worldwide. The site has a "Resource Center" with how-to instruction on various topics, such as applying rhinestone transfers or embellishing an old backpack. Good source for rhinestones, buttons, appliqués, ribbons, and accessories such as belt buckles, purse handles, feathers, frog closures, flower pins, sequins, pom-poms, tassels, and nailheads. 1008 Sixth Avenue (between Thirty-Seventh and Thirty-Eighth Streets), New York, NY 10018, 212-391-6200 and 800-965-8746. mjtrim.com
- Pacific Trimming—A New York City Garment District store with an excellent website, in English and Spanish. It has a wide selection of trims and hardware, including lace, cording, and fringe; high-fashion zippers; and specialty items such as handmade glass buttons. 218 W. Thirty-Eighth Street, New York, NY 10018, 212-279-9310. pacifictrimming.com
- Richard the Thread—Professional costumers buy grommet setters,

corset hooks, suspender buttons, and other supplies here. You may shop online or in the store. 1960 S. La Cienega Boulevard, Los Angeles, CA 90034, 310-837-4997 and 800-473-4997. richardthetread.com

- Sublime Stitching—Since 2001, designer Jenny Hart's creations have brought embroidery to an entirely new audience. Her company is "the original source for alternative embroidery," and it's a one-stop mail-order source for zippy patterns, kits, and supplies that go way beyond hearts and flowers. sublimestitching.com

- Tender Buttons—This citadel of antique and extraordinary buttons does not do mail-order, but it is well worth a visit. 143 E. Sixty-Second Street, New York, NY 10065, 212-758-7004. tenderbuttons-nyc.com

BOOKS

Antique Trader Vintage Clothing Price Guide, by Kyle Husfloen and Madeleine Kirsch (Krause Publications, 2006). Co-authored by the owner of the extensive C. Madeleine's Vintage Showroom in Miami, this illustrated guide includes comparable pricing for clothing, shoes, ties, hats, and purses, noting that vintage prices vary regionally in the United States.

Collecting Costume Jewelry, 101, 202, 303, by Julia C. Carroll (Collector Books, 2004, 2006, 2010) Three books of detailed and comprehensive price guides, photos, and history of costume jewelry. Written by a retired book editor, these out-of-print books are definitive but pricey, costing from $50 to $80 from online used bookstores.

Official Price Guide to Vintage Fashion and Fabrics, by Pamela Smith (Random House, 2001). Written by a knowledgeable collector, using prices from web-based and actual vintage stores. A well-illustrated history of fashion in the last century. Prices are from high-end, not thrift finds, but they are still useful for comparison today.

The Mood Guide to Fabric and Fashion: The Essential Guide from the World's Most Famous Fabric Store (Stewart, Tabori & Chang, 2015).

Entire chapters and color photographs devoted to cotton, linen and hemp; wools; knits; silks and other fabrics.

FASHION HISTORY

- American Textile History Museum—An affiliate of the Smithsonian Institution, this venue houses fifteen thousand clothing artifacts and a ninety-thousand-item Osborne Library of books and trade literature. Photographs and descriptions are searchable on its Chace Catalog. 491 Dutton Street, Lowell, MA 01854-4221, 978-441-0400. athm.org
- Kheel Center ILGWU Collection Archives—Cornell University's collection of items representing the history of the International Ladies Garment Union Workers, which includes label samples by date. ilgwu.ilr.cornell.edu/archives
- Irene Lewisholn Costume Reference Library—This reference library is located within the Museum of Modern Art in New York City. Contains 1,500 designer files and 25,000 books and magazines on fashion history, regional clothing, and worldwide costumes from the sixteenth century to today. Access is limited and by appointment only on Tuesdays through Thursdays, 10 a.m. to 4 p.m., via e-mail at costumeinstitute.library@metmuseum.org. Browse the digital collection first, at libmma.contentdm.oclc.org.
- Wenham Museum—A collection of more than ten thousand pieces of clothing, accessories, and textiles from the Victorian age to today. 132 Main Street, Wenham, MA 01984, 978-468-2377. wenham museum.org

ONLINE FULL-PRICE RETAILERS FOR LABEL RESEARCH

- Farfetch—An e-commerce retailer carrying items from over 400 boutiques worldwide, focusing on designer clothes for men and women. Good editorial content. farfetch.com

- MR PORTER—A compendium of men's fashions from a wide variety of designers, with interviews on fit, style and design. mr.porter.com

DONATING CLOTHES FOR JOB RE-ENTRY

- Dress for Success—A worldwide charity with the goal of giving business clothing and career counseling to women and men in 150 cities and 20 countries. Learn how to donate clothes or volunteer at dressforsuccess.org

RECYCLING CLOTHES, GREEN FASHION

- 2ReWear—A textile recycling service in Clifton, New Jersey, that partners with retailers and cities to recycle unwanted clothes, shoes, and household textiles to reduce the 25 billion pounds of textile waste already in U.S. landfills. Participating online and actual stores give donors coupons for future purchases. 2rewear.com
- Clean by Design—The Natural Resources Defense Council's program to reduce water and other pollution in fabric dyeing and finishing urges consumers to wash clothes in cold water and avoid PERC-based dry-cleaning in favor of wet cleaning or carbon dioxide cleaners. Clean by Design works with retailers (Target, Levi, Gap, H&M) and designers like Stella McCartney to encourage best practices in textile mills. It focuses on regions, like Suzhou, China, with its six hundred textile mills, to cut environmental degradation. nrdc.org/international/cleanbydesign
- Ragfinery, a "textile transformation" nonprofit, is a textile reuse center in Bellingham, Washington, that offers classes in weaving, sewing, garment upcycling, and crafts made from recycled fabrics. It sells remnants, notions, and buttons and takes donations of unwanted textiles; it also offers low-cost consultations on alterations and combining or updating garments. ragfinery.com

acknowledgments

This book was helped by the assistance of many thrift store owners, the expertise of artisans in clothing and accessories repair, the thoughtful tips of dozens of avid thrift shoppers, and the creative help of the many women and men who modeled outfits.

The imagination, energy, and efficiency of our photographer, Roger Snider of Los Angeles, and his assistant, Kevin Pershin, made our long days of photo shoots possible. Our hair and makeup professionals were headed by Jayme Kavanaugh (jaymemakeup.com). Our models, who gave us the gift of their time and talents, were drawn from our families, friends, and co-workers. We warmly thank them all: Blake Berris, Yolander Biggs, Tyler Boudreaux, Hattie Confalone, Irina Escuadro, Greg Gainor, Alan House, Nora Kirkpatrick, Shirley Lau, Cristy Lytal, Christiahn Moore, Danielle Moore, Jordan Moore, Marzen Moore, Bryn Mooser, Devon Near-Hill, Stacey Torii, Richard Villegas, Katelynn Whitaker, and Sophia Winnikoff.

For various help and kindnesses, we thank Rachel Apatoff, Valerie Barreiro, Barbara Biggs-Lester, Ray Bolouri, Chelsea Confalone, Brian Darrith, Marla Eby and Goodwill of Southern California, Rachel Ericsen, Kim Garretson, Glen Howard, Pam Jones, Kobos Studios, Angela Lampe, Greg LaVoi, Natalie Malchev, David Mathias, Dave Mayer,

Anna Phelan, Dietmar Quistorf, John Rankin and Boomtown Brewery in Los Angeles, Michelle Raven, Joe Salasovich, Terry Salazar, Joyce Sobczyk, Charlotte Stratton, Todd Thelen, Ellen Warren, and Joan Warren.

Our gratitude, also, to publishing experts Ib Bellew and Carol Kitchel, who recognized the value of this book and introduced us to the creative team at Charlesbridge Publishing. And special thanks go to the exceptionally talented Joe Lops for his clear, creative design for this book.